Jesse is a Ghanaian conscientious writer, poet, political theorist and activist, who is an advocate for racial equality and global justice. He was born in the United Kingdom, his heritage sewn into the fabric of the royal Ashanti tribe of the Akan people. He regularly travels back to his motherland, Ghana. Having worked in the corporate finance world for many years and being educated in the United Kingdom, he has had first-hand experience of the perils of racism, assimilation and its adverse effects on black people; and more importantly its crippling impact on black potential. He seeks to unravel the psychology behind racism and to explore the power of manipulation upon the human mind, and hence its conditioning. He explores contemporary, as well as historical, political, psychological issues, particularly in relation to identity and stereotypes, in hopes of exposing false ideas that have been embraced globally about black people. Jesse, acknowledges that the re-education of the mind is central to the true emancipation of African descendants.

Thank you, my mother, for holding me and guiding me through the heinous winds and dark storms; thank you for showing me the true mirror image of my identity as a black man. And delivering and protecting me, for honouring me in my childhood, in watching me fall, watching me struggle for air and helping me to rise up; for watching me bleed, cry, and die in silence. For diligently praying for me and speaking to the heavenly spirit on my behalf. You have always been my anchor and for that, I bow down before you, my beautiful black queen, I honour you, and anoint you with my immortal love forever.

Jesse Yaw

THE DECONSTRUCTION OF HUMANITY'S VOICE, BUT WE ARE STILL STANDING

AUSTIN MACAULEY PUBLISHERS™

LONDON • CAMBRIDGE • NEW YORK • SHARJAH

A CIP catalogue record for this title is available from the British Library.

ISBN 9781398430181 (Paperback)
ISBN 9781398430198 (ePub e-book)

www.austinmacauley.com

First Published 2022
Austin Macauley Publishers Ltd®
1 Canada Square
Canary Wharf
London
E14 5AA

I would like to thank my family and loved ones for inspiring and encouraging me to write this book, and acting as a support during this process. Which is meant to foster trust and unity particularly amongst black people and the wider African diaspora. My mother once told me, your pen is your sword, and indeed I can see how the power of words can transform, not only a mind, but a generation to come.

The Psychological Creation
of Black Male Identity

As a black man, I have learnt that my ebony skin means more than my physical commonality with all human species in the global community – which encompasses all races and nationalities. My black skin is more than my voice, it is more than my hidden smile, it is more than my personality, it is more than my dreams, and it is more than my future. I learnt to be subconsciously afraid of the police, I learnt to be afraid of the law and the white man's order, I learnt to accept inequality as a norm, I learnt to worship white beauty, white governance and to assimilate. And I must confess, I learnt to put on that white mask, which became my natural umbrella, which allowed me to bridge and navigate the gulf that the perception of my dark charcoal skin created, and in this, I learnt to understand my place as a black man. But no more, I would rather speak up, educate and prepare the future black generation, than lose my position as a good house nigger, and to therefore assimilate and be silent, and die a death of mental enslavement.

So, my brothers, I must confess and I will be honest with you. In the possession of this black skin wrapped around your spirit, you will face adversity, you will face dishonour, you will face disrespect, you will face mental anguish, you will face physical abuse, you will face injustice, you will be moulded to hate yourself and to be subconsciously subservient. And therefore you will be angry. This experience will unfold all before you turn sixteen years old, just when you realise that yes, I am becoming a black man and that yes, the white man wants me inside their prison system, just like a statistic and just like the experience of our ancestors.

As black men, our power and the potential of the black race to lead, shake the cores of the white man's imperialism. Why does the white man want to break us? Why did he seek to castrate us as runaway slaves? Because united as black people we are unbreakable. As a black man, I have seen how psychological racial programming has painted the black specimen destructively, as an inferior sub-class species.

Why is the experience of the black male race so distinctive? What is most gripping about the creation of black male identity by the white race, is the creation of black identity as the lowest form of being in the global racial pyramid, if we can agree that there is a hierarchy among races, with the white race at the top. By this, I mean all other races and ethnicities of colour are also conditioned, to look down on black people as the most inferior race. Given that they have been hypnotised into this racially constructed pyramid. The unique facet about the creation of white racial superiority is its subconscious voice that permeates into the foundation of the human mind. In this, it conditions and designs the fabrics of our human racial interactions. The majority of the human races' minds have been programmed globally by the colonial narrative of social media, a tool controlled by the white race, who project colonial narratives about racial hierarchies, with the white race at the top of the racial pyramid.

It is only when we can deconstruct the voice of the powerful in this world, that we as broken black men can reconstruct our identities, and release and overcome the minefield of anguish and racial destruction that myself, that you, my brothers, and our children will face in this white man's world. And before you ask me, yes, I believe that we are broken black men because our identities are not whole, but rather loose reflections of our insecurities, our failures and anguish at our intentional marginalisation by the white man.

The truth, or our human truths is the agreement of an idea by the powerful in the world, the powerful in the world is the white race, a preeminent[i] race whose voice and ideas have largely shaped and conditioned the rest of humanity's voice. So how can humanity really know the truth, and discern fact from fiction? If the voice of humanity has been coloured by the ideas of the white man through centuries of colonial rule and violence, how can we as a black race know our identity, if our truths in our minds have been coloured by the power and echo of the white voice? The human mind is soft and sticky, and prone to conditioning through words, images, and the perception of morality. So who am I? And how do I continue to stand in my identity?

In the "truth", the white man bestowed upon me, you, our ancestors and humanity. I realised growing up that my identity as a black man was like a mark of death, a curse in ways unfathomable to me at the time of my young boyhood. I never understood or anticipated the hardship, pain and turbulence that I would experience as a young black man growing up in a racially hypnotised society, going to school in white-dominated areas, working for white western corporations, dating women of other races. I came to realise that these women of other races' minds were largely also conditioned by racialised Western programming, into the sexualised fetishisation of my black skin, using my dark melanin as a mechanism to rebel against their conceptions of normality. Or rather using my black skin as a tool for them to feel superior, rather than wanting me for the attraction of my personality or character. I become simply that, a mechanism to fulfil a purpose.

I remember, going on a second date with a girl from a European ethnic group, at the dinner table, with wide eyes, head tilted forward, with the most innocent and reassuring smile she asked me, "what would you like to order?" Before I could answer, she reassuringly mentioned: "I bet you will get the chicken, you always get the chicken, I don't know why that is." In fact, I had previously ordered the salmon and never ordered chicken, in her mind, I was ordering something typically associated with being black. Similarly, at a dinner party, I remember talking about employment opportunities with a Chinese girl, and she casually mentioned: "I hate going into interviews and seeing black people, you know they will get the job because of positive discrimination."

I found it interesting how people of other races, presupposed that it was okay to disrespect and behave prejudicially towards a race that I am a part of, as though I did not belong to that race. It is almost as though, if you as a black person, have met certain White Western "upper class" criteria (i.e. going to elite universities, going to private schools, working in certain "elite" places or institutions), in their psyche you are viewed as less "black" on the racial pyramid. Even dating a black woman in their psyche is viewed with confusion, they begin to wonder, why he is not with a white girl? As they believe they are superior, even entitled and more attractive than black women.

And therefore, you are viewed as though you are one of their subjects, and therefore they feel comfortable talking to you in a racist[ii] manner, as if being a black person isn't who I am or who you are. What I realised, underpinned all of these occurrences was the fact that, when they see black skin, there is a level of innate disrespect, and expectation that you should just adhere and not challenge their racist philosophies, if you do, you become the problem. The fundamental psychosis, if I may, in their minds is that you are a second-class citizen, and in fact, a black slave boy, you are even lucky that I am having this conversation with you. Now, you have graduated to house nigger status, therefore you are trusted with my innate racism, you are below me so you should not question my racism.

My people, in order for the white race to create our black identities, he must first focus on the parameters to define you, then he must understand your reactions to particular stimuli, we become a research project, an obsession, the aim to have full control. It is very similar to researching the behaviour of animals in the animal kingdom. First, an observer must understand what food the specimen eats, supposedly (fried chicken, watermelon), what form of entertainment we enjoy, supposedly (Jazz, RNB, gangster rap, hip hop). And finally, they start to develop a file based on how these facets of our identity can be used to shape us. To the extent that they anticipate how we act, talk, walk, and dress, these features become documented in their psyche. These racial parameters are used to define us, it becomes the skeletons of our identity, this narrative is fed into the media (news, movies, TV, screen plays, politics, and education), over centuries of massaging into the ecosystem of humanities subconscious, it becomes humanity's reality.

This creates a constructed mirror of identity (i.e. in current times, what I refer to as the Neo-Colonial Hollywood Mirror), where physical black skin transcends the white man's natural vision, rather his vision of black people becomes a subconscious constructed mirror, which dictates his thoughts with ideas espoused by centuries of prejudiced racialised ideology. The Neo-Colonial Hollywood Mirror is an identity creator, which is underpinned by three Western pillars (economy, policy and military). Contemporary Human identity can be written as a mathematical function, for example: (Identity = Neo-Colonial Hollywood Mirror÷economy, policy, and military).

The white man's psychology and vision becomes subdued with this subconscious mirror, built and passed down from generation to generation. So much so that when he creates literature, films, poems, policies, or trade, he becomes lost in this mirror. I call this the Neo-Colonial Hollywood Mirror because this is a psychological mirror, which has imprisoned the mind of the white race since colonialism. And this status-quo is refracted in racist ideology in current times through the media, and indeed social media, without humanity being aware that racism has become their subconscious masters, a disease.

It is clear to me that the white race owns and controls this Neo-Colonial Hollywood Mirror given that they invented it, this mirror is metaphysical in nature, and it shapes humanities subconscious, and programs human minds with the currency of its colonial voice, through the media and information technology. Other theorists have used terms such as soft power to allude to this. In this, the black man's identity has been psychologically manufactured, such that he is internationally perceived as the most inferior animalistic creature in the global human community.

During the early stages of film and media, black people struggled to represent their own stories, histories and beliefs, and identities because slavery eradicated and recreated a new identity for the black race in a post-colonial society. Importantly, whites controlled the entertainment industry (i.e. the Neo-Colonial Hollywood Mirror) and created the images of the black race that was portrayed to the world. The deals for the films were decreed by companies such as Columbia Pictures and the Motion Picture Association of America (Bausch, 2013)[iii], both of whom were established and controlled by white men. Dean Larry Davis from the University of Pittsburgh argued: "One of the most important things any group of people can do is to control the image of themselves." (Barlow, 2011).

In the earliest examples of television programming, such as Birth of a Nation in 1915 and the Tarzan series from 1932, black Americans were symbolised in the films as: "savage, ignorant, thieves, interlopers and potential rapists" (Luther et al., 2012, p.59)[iv]. Even early film depictions of black Americans were being played by white people, taking away their voices. White producers chose for their actors to paint themselves to look black, the ideology behind this was that black people were not intelligent enough to represent themselves. Only white people were intelligent enough to play black characters. And the subconscious message was that white people were in control of black people's identities and destinies.

The subconscious message to the global community was that the white race was the "ideal", and the only "competent" group to participate in mainstream media (Luther, et al., 2012). Barlow (2011)[v], Dean Larry Davis from the University of Pittsburgh noted that: "Overwhelmingly, White Americans learn about African-Americans not through personal relationships, but through images shown by the media. Unfortunately, Blacks too consumed these same images." This means that the white psyche and that of the global community is being conditioned to embrace a negative stereotypical identity of the black race, which became their inherent truths. A "truth" bestowed upon them by the voice of the white man, in his depiction of humanity.

When I look in the mirror, the image that my eyes refract to me has not been coloured by the original combustion and assortments of physical shapes and colours. But rather by the subconscious influx of shapes and colours, and in this, the subconscious programming of ideas that have shaped my mind. I realised that the white colonial depiction of stories, images on TV, concepts of right and wrong, had coloured the truth of my vision. When I saw black skin, I understood my mind had been hypnotised into western cultural assimilation, subservience. Immediately, the abundance of a greater number of black people became synonymous with less professionalism, and meant standards were decreasing, even African features became less desirable.

I wondered how it was possible for my mind to have become hypnotised by Western bias, without me even being aware. It became clear on reflection that my mind had been programmed by Neo-Colonial Hollywood Mirror reflections from social media, TV, radio, politics, which had portrayed the white race as arbiters of righteousness, arbiters of peace, law and order. Effectively a race immune from judgment, because our minds have been conditioned to believe they are the righteous race. I wondered if, in my mind, I subconsciously viewed myself as inferior, if this could be true, how would that affect my interactions with white people and people who looked just like me? What would this mental acceptance of subservience mean for my spirit, for my black consciousness? Assimilation to the white race.

For example, during the 1940s, the psychologists Dr Kenneth Clark and Dr Mamie Clark designed the "doll tests" to study the effects of racial segregation on children. This gave insight into the psyche of the black child, and the extent to which racial assimilation had taken control of the black child's mind. During their tests, they asked African-American children to chose whether they preferred black or white dolls. Their conclusion was that the majority of black children chose white dolls, which exemplifies the power of the Neo-Colonial Hollywood Mirror. This case study played an integral part in the Brown v. Board of Education of Topeka, 347 U.S. 483 (1954), which ruled against segregation in US public schools.

In the sixty years since the Brown V. Board of Education case. These consistent results of the experiment, act as evidence of the subconscious conditioning of the black child's mind by the white man, which has persisted long after colonialism and desegregation.

Centuries of imperialism has conditioned the psychology and subconscious of the white race into an illusion of racial superiority, the conditioning is so severe that the white race has emerged as a political organisation, its psychosis is the white superior psyche syndrome (i.e. the fabricated belief the white race is superior to all other races, and therefore they have the right to impose their will). The majority of the white race endorses this consensus, which creates – white privilege – with economic and social perks underpinned by adherence to this doctrine. This syndrome, once widespread and endorsed by the majority of white citizens and the global communities, becomes weaponised, whiteness becomes a weapon to be used against non-white people. As they believe they are superior and have the right to enforce their will upon subservient blacks, this innate psychological belief becomes a syndrome, once this psyche is supported and endorsed by Western institutions, what emerges as white privilege, emerges as a facet of white super power.

This syndrome has not developed from thin air, it has been historically constructed by the white man's successful military campaigns, invading other countries, raping and pillaging communities by military force. And thereafter, enforcing their will upon those conquered communities, similar to the Roman Empire and their army of legionnaires, and the pharaohs' ancient Egyptian army. All of whom eradicated tribes, recreated artificial borders, marginalised and enslaved groups of minorities. Similarly, the white race has been able to preserve their power through the ability to create black identities, which has stemmed from the institutionalisation of slavery, which is now underpinned by Western institutions.

The power of the white race is dependent on the willingness of its white citizens to place their racial interests above the personal interests they may hold. It is very similar to holding the most coveted position in the playground as the biggest, strongest, bully, and willingly being able to forsake this privilege to help other people less powerful. Now, because the white race has largely been hypnotised with the idea that they are superior to all other races, this lie has been repeatedly told to them from their childhoods, and therefore it has become their subconscious and ontological "truths". Lies repeatedly told, can become truths, particularly when the powerful in the world agree on them.

The white race can only maintain this white superior syndrome, if citizens of the body politic of the white race, continue to perpetuate and believe these racist historical lies. The antidote to the white superior psyche syndrome is for the white race to resign from its political party, and concede its addiction to the psychological disease of the white superior psyche syndrome, their rehab will be the re-engineering of their identities that is independent and clear of the inferiority of all other races. The first step is for the white race who have been afflicted by the disease to concede: "*I am a racist addict, my subconscious is conditioned on racism, and I do not want to be afflicted by this disease anymore*".

The progressive white man will then concede in a poetic fashion:

I am infected by the DNA of white imperialism, which has been passed down from generation to generation, like a flickering curse. The disease of my white imperialism has blinded my vision and morality. My subconscious is hypnotised into the illusion of my supremacy. My mind is numb and controlled by the imposition of racial constructs, that have come to programme the membranes and cells of my mind. Ask me what my white identity is, I can give you no answer. Ask me to define the identity of other races, I can give you semi-scientific, historical and racially prejudiced based truth. As my existence is predicated on imperialism. Can't you see without this, I fail to exist as a form of the human entity; my value becomes reduced to the harsh mirror that reflects my insecurities and pain. Please free me from the DNA of my white imperialism, and give me my humanity back. Forefathers, you have tricked us your Anglo-Saxon bloodline and tricked and hypnotised the majority of all other races in the world into believing the imperialism of our white skin. I am so structurally hypnotised, my subconscious has become a racist disease, which manifests itself in the interactions I have with other races. And I do not know how to revoke this racism from my psychology, help me to find an antidote to the infection of my DNA by the white imperial construct – the white superior psyche syndrome.

In a similar fashion, the black race must concede: *I am not inferior to other races, my subconscious is conditioned by the addiction of the identity the white man has created, and I do not want to be afflicted by that disease anymore.* It is only then that the constructed racial pyramid, with the white man at the top, can be broken.

The black race is hypnotised with the fear of their own reflections, fear of looking into the reality of their own abyss and identities because the black race has no identity, just fragments of former African tribal glory passed down through African folk tales and their pre-colonial past. Martin Luther King pushed for civil rights (i.e. to eradicate the use of separate public utilities, and schools from the superior ones reserved for whites; to eradicate discrimination in employment and housing, to give blacks the ability to fully

20

exercise their right to vote). What he didn't understand was that the rights he was pushing for were the rights the white man had created, and within this window of rights, the black race didn't exist. In fact, for these rights to exist, it was dependent on racial inferiority, the black race being subservient.

In his infinite wisdom, his view of racial co-existence was the black race assimilating to the white race in order to gain their liberties, the problem which he realised later in his campaign was that this approach instantaneously placed the black race in an assimilatory bubble, below the white race, chasing the image and likeness of the white man, as though they were Gods themselves.

The black race has consequently laid in infancy, dependent on the white man to shape their consciousness and truths, black consciousness was most recently alive with the Black Panther movement, which was formed to challenge police brutality against the African-American community. But it became muted by a few of its members who wanted to assimilate to the American dream and the consequence of the brutal reality of death and imprisonment. The first FBI director, J. Edgar Hoover, in 1968 called the Black Panthers, "One of the greatest threats to the nation's internal security."[vi]

My people, we need to understand, the concept of the American dream does not exist for the black race. In this dream, if you look closer, you will see you're a slave. So black race, you are only a slave if you believe the illusion the white man has created for you, for in his eyes you will always have black skin, and he will always be your master.

The destructive psychological effect of being a black man, and being perceived as the most inferior type of human organism that roams the earth in its human form is powerful and poisonous enough for us, as black men to want to assimilate to the white race, embracing the distorted identity, which the white man in his efforts to control black people, has created. As a consequence, the majority of black men have fallen into the assimilatory trap of unconsciously trying to re-create their inferior black identities, into the likeness of their subconsciously perceived superior identity – the white man.

Similar sentiments have been echoed by anti-racist activist Christopher Day, who argued that "the grip that whiteness has on the consciousness of the majority of people in this society is an immediate and persistent obstacle to building any serious movement for radical change in this country. It is not a simple matter of doing the right thing, because whiteness obscures in our minds what the right thing is."[vii]

Being accepted in Western human society means following the rules and codes, stipulations set out by the white social class, in real terms following norms (i.e. rules and supposed norms). This creates a sense of human comfort, a form of programming of the mind that allows for governance and perceived order. However, I acknowledged that the idea of being accepted in Western society was measured against my propensity to look and act white. Particularly, when my aspiration was to get a good job, which would afford me the benefits of acquiring white wealth or Western capital goods (a car, a house, designer clothing).

So I learnt to speak the way the white man spoke, I learnt to write the way the white man wrote, even the image of Jesus Christ to this day in my mind is linked to a white man with long hair and white skin. I wore their shoes, their suits, their jackets, their chinos, and their shirts. All materially linked items of the white upper class, in pursuit of attaining the white man's likeness, and hence respect, in their subconscious I knew they would be thinking: "he is a decently dressed black boy," "oh he's alright," effectively the black guy that gets a pass, which gave me a sense of comfort. But I began to question how this concept of "decent" and how its suitability was arrived at. It was the psychological hypnotisation driven by the Western media, of what my concept of acceptance, the norm, and decency was.

This is exactly why assimilation to the white race has been a key tool, the white man has used to foster racial inferiority of the black race in the mind of the black man. The aim, subconscious submission, and desire to attain and mimic white forms of social and cultural society. The power of assimilation is underpinned by perceived moral and economic superiority. In this, assimilation to the white race is perceived as the formula to a superior economic and moral mode of existence. This blueprint of white racial-cultural assimilation is projected onto the global community, through propaganda from internationally dominant Anglo-Saxon run media outlets, which have the effect of programming the minds of citizens of the global community. This programming of the mind, creates an assimilatory narrative (i.e. the white race as superior and the other non-Anglo-Saxon races as inferior). Assimilation as I define it is a racialised psychological hypnotisation, reinforced by the seduction of potential perks of white economic and social superiority. And the attainment of success is defined against the measure of elite white social society.[viii]

I have seen that the neo-colonial identity creation of the black man by the white man, has reduced the identity of the black man to the confinements of his struggle to be free from enslavement, and within this, the pursuit of an economically superior life. My people, it is important to realise that poverty is the devil, which has kept the large majority of the black race locked in a prison cell, our creativity, our happiness, our independence shackled against the inability to provide for ourselves, our families and to survive.

The black race in modern times, has experienced racial trauma on levels not seen since the oppression of the Israelites by the ancient Egyptians. The current black racial experience is a response to post-traumatic stress gained by severe historical oppression (i.e. Jim Crow laws that enforced racial segregation, and the Home Owners Loan cooperation act, which left black communities' poor – to name a few policies that institutionalised racism). This is the trigger that feeds the need to assimilate to the white man, his laws, his governance, his economic structures, his food, his wine, his clothes, his hair and his skin. Given the potential of economic perks, or at least the experience of having a slice of white privilege. This pursuit of the superior economic life is the – materialism and luxuries linked to white social status – that the white man has created for all the "inferior" non-white races in the global community to aspire to possess.

Now based on these parameters, there are two problems that emerge, with the identity of the black race (i.e. to be free from enslavement and the pursuit of an economically superior life): (1) it instantly puts the black man in opposition to something or an idea, and begs for such parameters of this opposition to be defined by a superior other (i.e. the white race), and (2) it moulds the identity of the black man into his pursuit of attaining white western capital goods, and in this, in order to attain such goods, it necessitates racial assimilation to the white race. Therefore, the black man is left similar to a child chasing a kite across the desert, and becomes lost.

My brothers, I want us to acknowledge that the racial engineering of the identity of black men, since the post-colonial era by the white man, stems from the eradication of his African black identity during slavery. Current tribal conflicts seen in Africa, since post-colonialism in African states, is a result of arbitrary post-colonial boundaries drawn by the white man, which forced various black tribal communities to live within artificial borders, which created a misplacement of their black identities, effectively an "identity vacuum".

This "identity vacuum", allowed the white man to re-create black identities and embed hatred within black identity constructs. For example, the Hutu and Tutsi conflict which stemmed from the Berlin conference of 1884, with Rwanda and Burundi being assigned to Germany who favoured the Tutsi over the Hutu when assigning administrative roles, given their parity in European physical features, believing them to be migrants from Ethiopia, a country identified as racially superior by the white man, given their lighter skin complexion.[ix]

This conference acted as a mechanism by which African identities were divided, re-created within artificial state borders. In order to create a racial pyramid, which allowed for the eradication of black identities. And full economic and physical control over Africa's resources, Uzoigwe notes that: "Bismarck ... stated in his opening remarks that delegates had not been assembled to discuss matters of sovereignty either of African states or of the European powers in Africa." It was no accident that there were no Africans at the table – their opinions were not considered necessary. The efforts of the Sultan of Zanzibar to get himself invited to the party were summarily laughed off by the British. The underlying psychology of the white man is, we are superior, we have and will continue to define African identities and futures, and you are insignificant.

Before Western colonialism, African nations were characterised by fluid identities and cultures. The white man needed to break these identity structures such that they could create, control and understand the Africans. As Terence Ranger noted, the partitioning of Africa was underpinned: "by systematic inventions of African traditions – ethnicity, customary law, 'traditional' religion. Before colonialism Africa was characterised by pluralism, flexibility, multiple identities; after it, African identities of 'tribe', gender and generation were all bounded by the rigidities of invented tradition."[x]

"The Berlin Conference was Africa's undoing in more ways than one," wrote Jan Nijman, Peter Muller and Harm de Blij in their book, Geography: Realms, Regions, and Concepts. "The colonial powers superimposed their domains on the African continent. By the time independence returned to Africa… the realm had acquired a legacy of political fragmentation that could neither be eliminated nor made to operate satisfactorily."[xi] Here it is clear that not only were black African identities eradicated but any form of political governance post colonialism would be hindered.

During World War One, Belgium took direct control of Rwanda. In 1935, Belgium introduced identity cards which institutionalised the white racial hierarchy into black identities, you were either Tutsi, Hutu, Twa or Naturalised. The identity cards prevented any social class movement between the black identities, the white man had created[xii]. This resulted in 85% of Rwandans being Hutus, however, the Tutsi minority had gained dominance in the country, due to the positions and seats that were given to them by the white man. This seed of racial identity eradication, embedded racial hatred that the white man engineered and sewed into Rwandan identity constructs centuries ago, resulting in the 1994 Rwandan genocide, 100 days of tribal killing resulting in over 800,00 deaths.

Introduction

"The media's the most powerful entity on earth. They have the power to make the innocent guilty and to make the guilty innocent, and that's power. Because they control the minds of the masses" – Malcolm X.

The inability to unite is the demon that keeps the descendants of Africa's children divided, repression is the mad angel that has kidnapped the imagination of the black race, and assimilation is the red violin that has muted black self-determination.

As black men, our identities have been socially constructed before we were even formed in our black mother's wombs, by the forefathers of the white man. Centuries of racial engineering, centuries of oppression, the purpose of which is to stifle black human progression. And to thereby enhance and maintain white racial superiority. The current voice of Humanity is the "voice" of the white man, as his perceptions and ideologies have been embraced by the global community as "truths". By the voice of the white man, I am referring to widely accepted social norms and ideas on class and human characteristics.

From this "voice", identities, including black identities were born. This voice has developed into prejudice, and is now a racial psychosis, what do I mean by racial psychosis? I mean that this has developed into insanity, caused by a psychological disease, not passed by human interaction or by molecules in the air, but by the hypnotisation of hatred upon the black race, and the racial conditioning of the mind through social media and the persistent televising of black inferiority[xiii]. This insanity is what I call the disease that has hypnotised the global community[xiv] with black prejudice, that which has emerged as the white superior syndrome. Its addictive elements are like the power of addiction to cocaine, heroin or alcohol. It is so powerful it has come to psychologically hypnotise the minds of the majority of citizens in the global community, into internalising this prejudiced racial illusion, as an unshakeable truth.

As you unravel my thoughts and interpretations on black identity creation, you must be aware of the aim of my voice. I am not writing this piece to demonise the white race or to blame them for a lack of black progression as a race. Rather, I am writing this piece to cleanse the black race of its hypnotic addiction to the identity that the white man has created for him. The consequences have been the mental imprisonment of the black man, and the destruction of his vision and identity of himself. In order for future black men to understand who they are, they must follow me on this journey of the deconstruction of humanity's voice and partake in the reconstruction of the black male identity.

Information Technology Hegemon – Anglo-Saxon Identity Creation Tools

The power of Information Technology (the internet and social media) has become a preeminent force in the programming of black minds. It echoes Neo-Colonial Hollywood stereotypes about the black man, largely because this Information Technology has been built by the white man, who is afflicted by racial prejudice, victims of the white superior psyche syndrome.

In current society, the United States is an IT hegemon[xv], given its domineering global corporations (Microsoft, Amazon, Google, Apple, Instagram, Twitter, Facebook, Snapchat, Cinema, Newspapers, Television Networks and Media Outlets). I call them Information Technology hegemons because they control the majority of the markets, businesses, and platforms that operate and refract the ideas and identities of black people. These Information Technology outlets are Western Neo-Colonial Hollywood Mirrors that help to perpetuate colonial narratives, opinions about black people and consequently impact the harsh realities of black lives. For example, the new wave of white IT hegemony, facial recognition, has been buttressed by what is referred to as "techno-racism", because of its propensity to be used by law enforcement to biasedly imprison more black people.

This was highlighted by Willie Burton, a black man who was a member of the civilian Detroit Police Commission, he noted that Detroit's population is 83% black: "This should be the last place police use the technology because it can't identify one black man or woman to another," he said. "Every black man with a beard looks alike to it. Every black man with a hoodie looks alike. This is techno-racism." Not surprisingly at a July meeting on the issue held by the police commission over facial recognition, officers temporarily jailed Willie Burton for his protest against facial recognition[xvi].

Possessing IT hegemony is a weapon, whatever state has hegemony[xvii] over IT can shape perceptions, ideologies, and identities. My opinion is that currently Western states, primarily the United States and to a lesser degree the United Kingdom are predominantly IT hegemons, who possess the power to create the other and consequently their identity. It should therefore not surprise you that in the United States attempt to stem China's rise to super power status, they have begun targeting Huawei and branding it a national security threat to the United States. What underlies this is the ability of Huawei to catapult China to IT Hegemon status, displacing the US's ability to shape perceptions, ideologies, and racial identities – eliminating its powerful neo-imperial identity creation tools, which gives the white man the ability to shape and direct morality.

Understand my brothers, Information Technology through its corporate tentacles i.e. Twitter, Instagram, Facebook, Snapchat, these social media apparatuses, which are, on the one hand, outlets that allow freedom of expression, and artistic thought which we celebrate. Yet, on the other hand, they can be used to misguide, sway public opinion and be used as an extension of the Neo-Colonial Hollywood Mirror. Particularly, when it projects negative images about ethnic minorities and stereotypical colonial fabrications.

Indeed, without the inferiority of the black race, the white race has no identity, as its social construct is based on superiority. Further, these social media tools are arguably a reflection of the empty Western capitalist society. That which is underpinned by assimilation to white social classes, within which the global community electronically exists. An empty vacuum filled with white capitalist vanity and reflections of pictures filled with false white idealisations of what the white man deceitfully wishes to project to the global community.

Therefore, the Neo-Colonial Hollywood Mirrors help to numb the white man's pain, it helps to provide another superior identity that shields his vulnerabilities and insecurities, his reality. Similar to drug addiction to heroin or cocaine, social media creates an empty vacuum, a magician's wand and a smoke screen that allows escapism from the self, one's original identity and reality. This window is underpinned by the psychosis of the white man, and his need to feel superior to others through the social construction of false identities via social media, media, law, and policies. Imperialism is the white man's opiate, without this social construct, they cease to exist.

Indeed, these colonial reinforcing apparatuses have been used to negatively create the black identity with negative connotations and images, being consistently socialised and normalised, with black-ism. Even black comedians have made careers out of repatriating these neo-colonial idealisations of a black man.

Like the shape of an irreparable decapitated empty paper bag, the white man has devoured the sanity and identity of the black race. With one gentle stroke of his nationalistic red, blue and white paint brush, the white man has drawn on a woven crown of thorns to sit on our black heads like the sacrificial lamb, and plastic crowns and political and economic chains around the necks of black African leaders since post-colonialism. Ensuring with one humble stroke of the paint brush not to totally dilute the perfect slave auction piece, which sits controlled and bound by fear, subtly beside Uncle Sam's feet, below his foot rest.

In the same way, in 1900, Sir Frederick Hodgson, the Governor of the Gold Coast which is now Ghana, demanded to be allowed to sit on the Ashanti Golden Stool that encapsulated the spirit and identities of Ashanti peoples, living, dead, and yet to be born[xviii]. This act represented the control that the white man wished to stamp on the psyche of the black man, since the colonial era, and is reflective of such trajectories in present times.

The Black Man's Reality About the Pursuit of White Wealth

Sometimes, it is the inability of the black man to acknowledge that his consciousness has been robbed, which scares me. A black man will look at a black child with potential, and destroy that black child, by giving him ill advice, misdirecting him, and seeking to have full control over that black child, because he is aware that there is no father figure. And because he knows that the child is vulnerable, and he can take advantage of that child, by enforcing his own imperialism over his own black subject. In this instance, he is fulfilling his Massa duties, by perpetuating the spiritual chain of enslavement. That he is at times, not even consciously aware he is doing. The ideology is that, if I have been broken by the white man, I must also now break you innocent black child.

But he dare not touch a white child, for the fear of a subconscious lynching. With black skin, you will be frustrated by the white man or antagonised in a multitude of ways, because humanity through the Neo-Colonial Hollywood Mirror is taught that there are no consequences for the mistreatment of black people. The subconscious psyche that lingers on the global community is that no one cares, and unfortunately, there is a strong truth to this, as we are not viewed as human beings but animals.

You ask yourselves, why would a black man want to destroy another black child? This is because he is an agent of the white man. And he will sacrifice his own black sons to be accepted by them, if only for him to become a modern-day house nigger, rather than a modern-day field nigger. This happens because the black man has lost his identity, the white man has taken full power, and the pursuit of white social class status is all that drives him. The power of the white man, lays in their Neo-Colonial Hollywood Mirror, and its ability to brainwash black men. If in 500 years' time, our future black bloodline looks back on the way, we as current day black people are destroying and killing each other, they will weep.

But they will weep because they do not understand that our minds have been mentally enslaved. Imagine, the white man has pillaged and stolen from our African countries for centuries, yet within the global racial human species, he is the species we (humanity) all fear the least, and in fact, we allow him to come back and pillage and steal more, all with a smile on our faces. Our minds have been hypnotised and brainwashed, we accept subservience as a mode of operation, we black men will destroy another black man, all so that he doesn't rise above us in this racial pyramid. All so that we can attain even a fraction of white wealth and perceived esteem.

The reality of social media platforms is that they are controlled and owned by the white man, the global human community are hypnotised by the Neo-Colonial Hollywood Mirror, which projects racial biases, conditioning and shaping human minds. Our self-grandeur attempts, at showing our wealth and esteem is what the white man wants us to do on social media. Why would the white man want you to do this on social media? Because the idealisation of attaining the white man's luxuries will keep you blinded in the Neo-Colonial Hollywood Mirror, and in the constant pursuit of working harder only to become a house nigger instead of a field nigger, because we are playing into the hands of the white man's racial pyramid. That is, the attainment of things associated with white social class status, which reinforces white superiority.

The white man will never respect or see us as equal, no matter what we attain in wealth, riches, shares, properties or endorsements you are still a black nigger in their fabricated conditioned white superior psyche syndrome inflicted minds, bound and limited by Massa. Sometimes it surprises you when white people from a station that you perceive to be lower than yourself in rank: economically, academically or professionally, still look down at you and don't respect you. It is simply because you are playing the white man's game, which he has invented, you cannot change, bypass, cheat or recreate the racial pyramid.

The Neo-Colonial Hollywood Mirror isn't physical in nature, it is psychological and it affects the way we as human beings view each other. For example, mental associations, such as skin colour and material items allow the human mind to instantly associate and affiliate, qualify, professionalism through the programming of the mind, through the media and education. Albeit it has physical pillars and tentacles (i.e. the police, the rule of law, the military, medicine, politics, education, philosophy, and finance), you must remember one thing, all of the above is administered by the white man, and consciously controlled by him.

As we have acknowledged, the Neo-Colonial Hollywood Mirror is metaphysical and has subconsciously built and defined the norms of current-day social ideology. It is very similar to inventing the sport of basketball, inventing the rules, inventing the language, inventing the business, and expecting you who is the black bystander in the audience, to come off the stands and onto the basketball court in a heated match, and expecting to completely change the rules at your insistence, just because you as one black man in the crowd perceive the rules to be unfair. This can only be challenged or changed by creating your own rules and your own game.

Our ancestors, our grandparents, mothers, fathers, aunties, and uncles fought for change. Martin Luther King, Malcolm X, Nelson Mandela, sacrificed their freedom for black liberation. We had a black president Barack Obama who has come and left the White House, and like the cyclical curse of death, nothing has fundamentally changed, except a few liberties. Why is this? Why are black men being systemically killed, falsely imprisoned, perceived as drug dealers, gangsters and we are suffering in workplaces for equal pay and the same rights as our white counterparts?

It's very simple, if the black man's idealisation of success is linked to the idealisation of the parameters that the white man has pegged for our success as black men, we will never break free from our chains. What we have to understand is that it is all linked – your identity is linked to yourself, you are aware of yourself because of the other who is different to you. Now if you and your identity are organically linked to your self-determination, but the link is broken because your self-determination is subconsciously influenced by your Neo-Colonial Hollywood Mirrored idealisation of your black identity, you can never move forward or be free. You will remain in a state of hypnotic dormancy and infancy, which the black race has laid still and trapped in for the last few centuries.

White Brand Names
Language and the
Colonial Mirror

The appeal of brand names, use to be of interest to me because of the quality and also more importantly, what it evoked and represented about me. I wanted to be viewed as something of quality and position, therefore wearing expensive pieces of clothing, gave an illusion of outward wealth. It was the psychological pursuit of an idea or a perception of status, we wanted to project. I remember as a young child, waiting anxiously for the latest pair of designer sneakers to be unveiled, so I could acquire, and project what I thought was cool at the time. These perceptions impact how we treat people with different elements of brand clothing, in our minds we say "she must be rich" from seeing a bracelet or watch, without understanding how she got it, for example, it could have been donated, passed down, stolen or borrowed etc.

Indeed, even characteristics become associated with this. He is being flashy, when he wears too many designer goods, showing the label, what is he trying to prove? It looks trashy comes into the psyche. The concept of money not being able to buy class, this concept is interesting, it begs the question, what are we innately defining class against? For me, this class is measured against the identity of white social class, white wealth and white luxury goods, reserved for those deemed "elite", or rather the "white upper class".

During the transatlantic slavery era, what was referred to as Negro Cloth was far more than cloth in a black slave's world, it symbolised the mechanism by which the slave could navigate and project a different identity, which was closer in likeness to Massa. During the eighteenth-century period, most slaves were clothed in fabrics imported from England and Germany. Textile mills in England produced cheap cloth, most slave clothing was made from cheap linen.

The ideological power of fabrics, and what they meant was important to black slaves, many accounts describe slaves going barefoot during the week. Black slaves wore what was perceived as their "Sunday best" and on the walk to church, they would stop to put on their shoes before going into the church. Sunday services were a time to worship but also a time to see slaves from neighbouring plantations. Clothing became a window, by which the enslaved could emulate their Massa and their white families. Slaves were able to assert themselves as members of the fashionable world, a world controlled by their white Massa's. This acted as a temporary form of identity, the colonisers had created in order for slaves to aspire to. Particularly, during Sunday church services, where black slaves could pray to images of a white Jesus Christ.

Slaves used their free time doing the extra work required to make attire similar to their slave owners, using any disposable income to acquire nicer clothing. Slaves would spend Saturdays washing themselves, such that they could appear their best for church.

Clothing for black slaves was a symbolic feature from the transition from boyhood to adulthood. In the 18th and early 19th centuries, boys received short trousers, between the ages of 5 to 10. By the 19th century, this transition from boyhood to adulthood was marked by wearing long trousers. It is important to recognise that the period of boyhood was extended for black men, as many of those interviewed by the Works Progress Administrations Federal Writers Project between 1936 and 1938, indicated they were adult males and working in the fields before they received long trousers.

This had a deep psychological impact on black men in that period and allowed the white man to control the manhood and identity of the black man. Similar to the act of castration, black men became emasculated by the white man. Girls usually wore long dresses to symbolise womanhood between the ages of 10 to 13. Female transition into womanhood was often indicated by the start of a girl's menstrual cycle. On female plantations, slaves wore the clothing of adults earlier than boys. This was driven by the slave owners desire to reap more profit and to increase the enslaved population, by forcing slave girls to produce more slave children. In the 17th and 18th century enslaved men and women who wore shoes were given styles similar to those worn by white servants. This reinforced social white class, and the assimilatory racial pyramid. With the black slave in pursuit of the white man's material goods.

In current times, within the Neo-Colonial Hollywood Mirror, brands and clothing represent the ascent of social class. This social class is linked to the idealisation of the racial pyramid the white man has created in his Neo-Colonial Hollywood Mirror. In this, clothes emerge as a facet of identity creation. This is also paralleled on the macro level whereby the hierarchical identity amongst nation-states, become linked to psychological brands and psychological clothing such as: "great power", "super power" and "nuclear power", (i.e. this inclusion of a nuclear weapon, hypersonic missile, with the identity of a nation-state increases their position on the nation-state pyramid, whereas terms such as "rogue states", "failed state" decreases their position on this pyramid).

Linked into this is the idea of nation-sates, remember western governments are a collection of people, therefore it should not surprise us that this collection of individuals on a national level, when representing their states, get judged by the same racial profiling that we as individuals experience. I can see parallels between the (micro) human racial hierarchies, which is projected onto the (macro) nation-state hierarchy. Whereby white Western states are pinned at the top of the nation-state hierarchy and thereby possess this righteous hegemon global complex to enforce their will upon "weaker", "ethnic", "less developed", and "emerging markets" nation-states, references to Trump's suggestion that these other nation-states were "shithole countries".

Similarly, on a human level, clothing becomes an institution that psychologically allows for social mobility in one's mind. The interesting thing about clothing as it pertains to the black race is that within this, a sub-class is created by the white race, "he dresses like he is black," "he has an urban look," "he is wearing dark clothing and a hoodie," "these are the things that black people wear." It is used as a way to create parameters to define the black man. The black race has viewed and internalised this sub-class as a form of black fashion, but they have forgotten that these sub-class identities are the exact tools the white man uses to manipulate the configuration of our identities. For example, the historical propensity for fashion to elevate the black race has developed from the psychological indictment that the black race is inferior. This relates to current black fashion, which stems from subconscious elements of deprivation, with the free black man, now needing to espouse white upper-class social status, wealth and power through clothes.

By investing financial resources in chains and designer clothing, all of which is underpinned by a desire to be seen. A desire to invert the psychology of the white man, with their association of black skin with inferiority. What you will realise is that the more, you try to espouse perceptions of wealth to get closer to the idealisation of white upper social class, the more the white man will create different barriers to critique your attempts. Now too much gold on black skin looks trashy, now too many designer clothes mean he/she is poor. Now the black man with the expensive sports car must be a drug dealer, a footballer or it must be stolen. All of these subconscious indictments will play on your psyche and is informed by the Neo-Colonial Hollywood Mirror.

Suits have psychologically, emerged as symbolic organs which represent formality, professionalism and class. So much so, every modern leader with the exception of a few, have worn suits during their terms within government. Even black civil rights leaders (Martin Luther King, Malcolm X, Kwame Nkrumah), who led movements against white supremacy, adopted such clothing to affect their audience and subconsciously reflect white status and class. The question becomes, why innately did black leaders feel the need to wear suits? Where does this psychology derive from? We must concede that it derives from the need to represent and assimilate to white upper-class status, whether one is subconsciously or consciously aware. Immediately, the psychological idealisation of a suit equates to professionalism and class, this is derived from the conditioning of the mind, through the Neo-Colonial Hollywood Mirror.

Wearing suits, historically derived from the bourgeoisie, namely the Royal Court in Britain. Social class was institutionally reinforced through legal orders that inhibited, "commoners" from wearing "the royal purple", wearing high-quality furs, satin and velvet. These types of clothing were meant to be reserved only for courtiers or royals. These laws remained in place until the middle of the 17th century. With the onset of the Black Death in 1665, which caused economic and social strife. The extravagant clothing of courtiers put the monarchy at risk. Therefore, a new less extravagant dress code led to the creation of the modern suit. [xix]

It is interesting, the Rubik facets of identity creation of black gang culture (i.e. slang words, post code wars and associated clothing – bandana's, handshakes, walking in a particular fashion, gang signs etc.) Were engineered by the white man in his Neo-Colonial Hollywood Mirrors to perpetuate and glamourise a distorted identity of black men. The white man even went further, by engineering a sub-class black language that stemmed historically from the elimination of education for black slaves (i.e. historically forbidding black slaves from reading) and black African migrant language (i.e. Africans speaking broken English, what is now referred to as pigeon language – given English was a second language).

This emerges as a sub-class of English, which the white man has inspired and perpetuated. This creates a cultural-linguistic identity, which fosters an inferior linguistic sub-class for black people. These sub-class language barriers, for some black people, are seen as "cool" or fashionable within black social settings. This "black" sub-class of language is even used as a representation of "blackness" not speaking in this manner makes you "not or less black", (i.e. how black you are, becomes determined by how well one adopts this black sub-class of language, or in the African-American context keeping it real). Yet, subconsciously the black race is unaware that these slang words or that which become typified by the white man as "black words", "black language" or "black slang" creates a subconscious racial linguistic inferiority in relation to sound, accent, to the subconscious human psyche, which appears harmless.

Until, when you understand that these sub-class inferior black linguistic interactions engineered by the white man within his Neo-Colonial Hollywood Mirror, means black children underperform in state exams, they cannot express themselves in court to defend themselves against false accusations, they cannot secure jobs in interviews, even on the playground as black children, they do not have the language tools to communicate to their class mates if they are upset about something. In real terms this means the black child results to violence, rather than expressing himself through words, because he cannot express his ideas, he has less confidence, because of his linguistic inferior sub-class language, subconsciously he is kept trapped in a black box, which reinforces the colonial racial pyramid.

This also parallels black street fashion, for instance, wearing hoodies, particular sneakers and dark clothing, "low batty trousers", "gold teeth", "hoodies", "black balaclavas". Is seen as black fashion, what is interesting about this black fashion is that it creates a black sub-identity, whereby in the Neo-Colonial Hollywood Mirror, this black street fashion, creates an identity parameter that the white man defines, so much so that his police officers, use this as a basis to shoot unarmed black youths, this is like a self-fulfilling genocide.

This black street fashion is invented by the white man within the cusps of his Neo-Colonial Hollywood Mirror, the linguistic inferior black language, you speak in the "hood", or on "endz" or in the "borough," "city" or "gang", has been created and engineered by the white man for you to create the parameters for the police to target you, and in their subconscious, register you as a criminal to be imprisoned or killed. It is interesting how the black individual believes that this sub-black language, black street fashion is something invented and controlled by themselves, we are just blind.

In this, it should not surprise you, when a white person is surprised when you as a black individual have the ability to express yourself with confidence and are intelligent. As their white psyche cannot comprehend, how you are not afflicted by the black inferior linguistic trap. Instantly, their minds create other excuses to justify your "appropriate" "white like" speech, namely: "you grew up in a white area," "you got a scholarship to a white school or university," "you must be the son of an African president or diplomat," "you went to a private school." In the white man's subconscious mind, you are placed higher up in the black racial pyramid, because you are closer and more akin to his white style of speech.

Interestingly, would you believe me if I told you that global fashion brands were a part of the Neo-Colonial Hollywood Mirrors and that they were subconscious enforcers of racial white supremacy? Remember clothing is an expression of one's psychology, if our psychologies are skewed by the Neo-Colonial Hollywood Mirror, and if fashion brands are created to espouse white social wealth through visual branding, then this form of fashion is an enforcer of white class assimilation. For example, to put this in practicality, the Council of Fashion Designers of America only has 3% of its members who are black. For the Fall Winter 2019 New York Fashion Week, only 10% of the designers were black. Ask yourselves how many black African clothing brands are viewed as luxury global brands? The answer is none, why is this? It is because of the power of the Neo-Colonial Hollywood Mirror, and the ability of the white man to shape class, value and luxury within the cusps of their identity creating tools, in order to create assimilation.

Additionally, prestigious brands such as Gucci are being accused of profiting from blackface, representations of distorted black identity representations, which stem from slavery. Similarly, Moncler released a line that resembled the destructive Sambo stereotype. Katy Perry released shoes that resembled blackface. Prada produced an image of a black monkey with amplified red lips. Drawing parallel with "Sambo", used as a black identity creation tool in order to portray black people during slavery. In 1899, a children's book, "The Story of Little Black Sambo," helped solidify the derogatory images of dark-skinned children. The resemblance of which has since repeatedly been paralleled by high brand fashion labels over time[xx].

White actors would paint their faces black and leave large outlines around their mouths to imitate the image of black full lips. In the 1800s, blackface was used in minstrel shows. The purpose of which was to denigrate black identity and to portray black people as inferior or unintellectual. Minstrel shows formed a key part in shaping the white American and European views on race, it was a tool of the Neo-Colonial Hollywood Mirror, the aim to reinforce white superiority, by programming images of black lunacy and inferiority.

For example, in recent times Dolce & Gabbana was criticised for advertisements with stereotypes about Chinese people. Zara created a skirt with a character like Pepe the Frog, a figure embraced by far-right groups. Prada created bags with charms, a line called Pradamalia, which resembled black monkeys with oversized red lips. And the Swedish company H&M dressed a young black male model in a hoodie with the phrase "coolest monkey in the jungle," resulting in protests at South African stores[xxi].

It is interesting how these white-owned fashion labels, feel free to perpetuate images of racism. As it pertains to black identities, we must remember the black man in their psyche has no say in their identity creation, the white man is so blinded in the white superior syndrome that they fail to acknowledge any form of blatant racism. Remember in their psyche you are a black slave, and slaves have no voice.

My brothers and sisters, remember words form the fabric of human interaction, without words in our tool box our imagination and minds become trapped in an oscillating Neo-Colonial Hollywood Mirror. Thus, because the white man has created this inferior black linguistic language, he has the ability to control our minds and the identities that we have of ourselves. A simple reinforcement of the white Neo-Colonial Hollywood Mirror.

Let me ask, would we prefer to be a slave king of a black nation and answer to a foreign white power? Or would we prefer to be a free man or a poor state that can work to enrich and build relations with your black brothers and sisters, with other nation-states to your right and to your left? Remember, the white man is a simple thief, he stole our bodies, our identities, our gold, our diamonds, our governance, our hopes and visions, but never our spirits. Thieves are cheaters and when it is all said and done, cheaters never win the overall game. The question of how we overcome this robbery of our black race is up to us.

White Language Tools

I sit here, and I reflect back and wonder what the American dream really meant, and how this pursuit of freedom played into the Western capitalist system. It became clear growing up that these ideas were idealisations meant for the white race. Being black in western capitalist society, meant that we were programmed to fall in love with the idea, you can pursue and attain the same aspirations as the white man. But it becomes clear that this American dream is dependent on mass black inferiority, therefore these aspirations never become a full reality for black folk. Now within this dream, the white man does allow for dreams to come true, there will be a minority of blacks who will attain white upper-class wealth, this is enough to keep the black race dormant, in a constant state of an illusionary dream, and eyes shut. The black man will point and say look how that other black man or woman attained success, this "success" defined against the attainment of the white elite social upper-class. Remember, in order for a black person or the black race to fall in love with a dream, and never open their eyes. There must be proof that it is possible for that dream to be achieved by a black person. And indeed, there have been a handful of black men and women who have attained white "success". But what about the millions of other blacks who are still entrapped, by the economic, social and political trappings the white man has created? Only a fool would accept such a bargain, and fall in love with a white dream, which only allows a handful of blacks to realise this reality, and the majority of blacks to live, sitting with their eyes closed.

Anglo-Saxon white political notions such as the pursuit of freedom in the neo-colonial period, emerge as repeated white racialised propaganda projections to encourage assimilation to the white race. This is because, ideas of the pursuit of freedom, become psychologically reinforced drawings that the seemingly invisible white neo-colonial master had created in the black man's subconscious psyche. This was used as a means to allow the black race to adhere to white social class constructs, which is dependent on black racial inferiority.

Tied into this psychological slave mentality conditioning, is the existence of the white man as the righteous hegemonic "other," with the word white, being engineered to evoke psychological connotations of purity, sanctity, righteousness, decorum and order. By hegemonic, I mean the race which holds the most dominant and sort after position on the racial pyramid – the white race, so much so other races try to assimilate to that race in order to move higher up on the social class ladder. Even marrying into that race, such that they are perceived more favourably within the scale of the racial hierarchy. In this fashion, what I call a white righteous hegemon is created in the global human psyche, meaning communities of other non-white people and states, who assimilate to the ideology and ways of the white man, such that they can taste the white man's privilege. By hegemon, I mean a racial superpower, the white race, who uses the Neo-Colonial Hollywood Mirror to mentally program and condition the global communities' psyche. Which in the racial pyramid structure, pits the white man as a superior race at the top of the racial pyramid.

What underpins humanity's deception across the micro (human) and macro (nation-state level) by the white man is the creation of the Neo-Colonial Hollywood Mirror. This force plants the seed of the image of the white man as the superior "other" in the black man's psyche. This is repeatedly reflected through white racialised mirrors which are perpetuated in the media, through Hollywood, for example: (movies, radio, news, law, institutions, politics, philosophy, theatres and screen plays), which effectively becomes in modern times, what I call, the Neo-Colonial Hollywood Mirrors. As it reflects the historical black slavery colonial narrative (i.e. the black man as the inferior animalistic creature), and the white man as the righteous hegemon.

This white superior psyche syndrome largely underpins the majority of injustice that black men will experience in their lives, it ensures that the white man cannot view the black man as his equal or as a full human. In this way, the same rights or white privilege is not afforded to the black specimen, rather injustice, harsh treatment and death become psychologically internalised as a norm for the white man, when his idealisations and consequently his attitude towards the black race come into his psyche. The white superior psyche syndrome does not necessarily affect the entire white race, but the large majority of the white race is afflicted by this psychological disease, and this is played out in the injustice of court rooms, decisions relating to state aid, trade policies, and military intervention in civil wars. Right down to the micro-economic level, employment disparities, length of custodial sentences, who the white employee chose to serve first in a store, or whom a white homeowner or realtor selling or renting their property, chose to let to or sell to, based on racial prejudice and micro-aggressions. Or even getting your property valued for a house sale, or borrowing against your property, the white realtor or home valuer will give you a lower valuation, if they see that you have an African name, or a "black name," or black skin. For example, the New York times reported that Doctor Nathan Connolly filed a discrimination lawsuit because his home value increased by almost $300,00 after he removed his blackness from his house and loan application.

During my secondary school years, I went to a white-dominated school, where a high level of racist attacks was common place for people of ethnic minorities, particularly black students. On our way home from school, a family friend of mine took a different route, he was chased by a racist gang and had his head hit with an axe. Coming home every day meant avoiding this white racist gang on a daily basis, and there was no mention of this in the school assembly, even though there was an awareness of this white supremacy gang.

When on one occasion a group of black children banded together and charged at the racist gang, they were arrested by the police and the next day at school an assembly was held, to discuss the black gang that charged at the innocent white children, who were actually members of the white supremacy gang. For the five years at that school, I would walk through the grey corridors, where I was racially harassed and attacked, not once was there a mention of taking actions to prevent this. The one time blacks decided to defend themselves it merited the head teacher and an entire school assembly and the police.

The subconscious message in this was clear, white lives matter more than black lives. As a black student, I should just accept the injustice and abuse, as it is the norm.

It is only now as an adult, when I reflect on my teenage years, experiencing severe levels of racial abuse, in racist areas in the UK that I realised how strong the power of paranoia was upon me and black men more generally, the fear of being watched, the fear of being isolated, being not accepted and picked on. All these experiences created a shell, I had not acknowledged or accepted the trauma this caused on my identity as a young black man.

How Identity Creation
in Hollywood, Perpetuates
Black Identities

It is interesting to see which current day images, the Neo-Colonial Hollywood Mirror creates and projects. For example, in refractions of the white man, in current-day film motifs in Hollywood, the black woman leaves the abusive black man for the heroic and loving white man. The ideology created and socialised by the white man, of the black man being a greater lover than the white man is debunked.

This Neo-Colonial Hollywood Mirror has come to control the human global psyche. For example, neo-colonial mirrors reinforce 'white-washing' in movies and cinemas. Effectively, it allows the white man to re-create his historical identity over different ages, which masks himself as the superior race over the entirety of humanities history. Tied into this is the lens of the white man, who consciously and subconsciously suffers from the white superior psyche syndrome, which is his unwavering fabricated belief that the white race is superior to all other races and therefore has the right to impose their will.

In current slavery films, strangely the white slave owner falls in love with the black slave girl, and the black slave girl falls in love with the white slave owner. The reality of this is the black slave girl would have been brutally raped on a daily basis. And yet, somehow in the current Hollywood colonial idealisations, the white slave owner miraculously becomes her hero whom she falls in love with. These socialisations of the white man as a superior spouse is an attempt to eradicate and deform the identity and value of black men as lovers, husbands and fathers. Which is key to the eradication of the identity of the black family structure and the notion of a good black man.

In the Neo-Colonial Hollywood film industry, even the notion of the black man always dying first in the horror movie, although normalised and joked about by black comedians. This is a subconscious reinforcement and normalisation of the black man as the sacrificial lamb to the slaughter. It is subtle, but such widespread neo-colonial psychological messages facilitate the eradication of the black man, which becomes socialised in pop culture as a norm and becomes a realisation when we look at cases such as the killing of Trayvon Martin.

In the black superhero series such as Luke Cage, note that his heroism is limited to his black environment, he is not a universal superhero, he is Harlem's superhero. When associations of black heroism or black excellence abound, they seem to be always limited or caged by an idea or image created by the Neo-Colonial Hollywood Mirror, such as the black neighbourhood (white subconscious idealisations about black people as slaves on a cotton plantation and imprisonment).

Indeed, Harlem is a typically impoverished black neighbourhood, yet it is the backdrop of the Luke Cage series, it is a storyline that puts black villains against black villains, a reinforcement of black-on-black crime, note also the black protagonists' power is to be bulletproof, a gentle white allusion to fabricated notions such as: black on black gun crime and the 18th-century medical idea that black people have thicker skin than white people, and are thus prone to less pain.

Parallels can be drawn with this "bulletproof", ability, which alludes to endurance, thickness, animalistic strength similar to the created white ideology of the black slave. Luke Cage's ability isn't to teleport or fly which alludes to freedom, universal white power. But repetitiveness is made to his geographic station: "Harlem". Similar to the formation of "black elites", groomed to be the puppet kings of their black tribes and countries, in their impoverished neighbourhoods. This is also representative of Black Hollywood, never eclipsing or touching the superior White Hollywood, Black Hollywood staying in its station and lane.

Note also, the use of the word coffee an addictive temporal substance, a fetishisation linked to sexual encroachments, we can immediately see the parameters and limitations of this black hero, his heroism being limited by the social setting the Neo-Colonial Hollywood Mirror has created to reinforce, the black hero within the racial pyramid.

This draws similar parallels to the Black Panther film, with fascination drawn by the white audience, from its representation of tribal backward African practices, note that the anti-hero isn't the white colonialist, the anti-hero is a fellow black man, which plays nicely into the white psychological projection of black on black crime and irrational black African tribal civil wars, with the wider audience not necessarily being aware that historically, such civil wars were engineered by the white colonialist. Note that this secret world Wakanda, where an advanced black civilisation exists, in reality, it does not exist on planet earth, instead, the representation of the protagonist coming into American civilisation sets them in Harlem under the guises of drugs, and the Black Panther movement, which ultimately failed.

This again plays into the comfortable setting of the white man's psychology, a world in which blacks are technologically and economically ahead does not exist on this planet, but only in a fictional alien world. Note that at end of the film, the hero is at the UN giving a speech in a suit, note that psychologically in the white psyche this is an admission of defeat and assimilation to white hierarchical norms, and a reinforcement of the racial pyramid. The subconscious racial implication is that the UN, an Anglo-Saxon financed vehicle for the white man, enforces normality and law and order in the neo-colonial hierarchical order, which in reality, it is a farce multilateral institution at best. A reinforcement of the white man's righteous hegemony.

Indeed, the power of the black Wakandan people and their technological advantage stems from Vibranium, a rare metallic substance of extra-terrestrial origin. This parallels with the wealth of natural resources of current African nations, however, it also projects the calamity of Black African wealth. And the blood diamonds and theft that underpins, its inability to transfer poorer African nations into wealthier ones. Importantly, central to this is the reinforcement of the Neo-Colonial Hollywood Mirror. This tribal substance that makes Wakanda a technological ultra-power among states and is a tribal substance from extra-terrestrial origin, which is linked to a diamond purple glittered black panther. Alludes to subtle subconscious links to the concept of backward – Black African tribal voodoo practices. Black excellence here is limited by a fantasy; a fantasy the white man ends up controlling through his Western Institutions the UN.

The Concept of White Beauty and White Hollywood

My concept of beauty has been created and shaped by the Western media since I was a child, images of white women with long hair and fair skin, became the benchmark for beauty not just within my psyche, but within the global communities given the powerful projection of the Neo-Colonial Hollywood Mirror. Within this conditioning, the extent to which a black woman was viewed as desirable was the extent to which she could mirror the image of a white woman.

Unfortunately, in current day society, the majority of black women are forced to assimilate, and indeed wear wigs and weaves to be accepted in Western society. They are perceived in the Neo-Colonial Hollywood Mirror as the least attractive female race. And to this end, this has a deep emotional impact on the disposition and confidence of black women. Black women, in the same vein as black men with white women, become fetishised by white men too. If two black women are standing beside each other, typically the black woman who is closest to a white woman in terms of features and overall looks, within the Western media is perceived as more attractive than the black woman who has typical African features. During the colonial period, New Orleans and Charleston had what was referred to as the fancy trade, whereby mixed race and light-skinned black female slaves, who were perceived as more attractive than darker skin black slave women, given their likeness in complexion to white women. And were therefore sold specifically as concubines for wealthy white Southern men.

Many lived as mistresses in dwellings of men who also had a wife and children on plantations. Fine clothing was an aspect critical to the success of the slave traders who sold these victims – what was termed, fancy girls. In this, fine clothing or clothing traditionally designated for white women becomes an expression of exploitation, for black female slaves. Slaves who worked in the slaveholder's house had better clothing than fieldworkers, to project their elevated status. Indeed, slaves who worked in the house of the slave owner (house niggers), looked down upon slaves who worked in the fields (field niggers), their clothing became a tool that morphed into their identities, emerging as a force that enforced black on black inferiority complexes. The hope, of the black slave of being able to emulate this white clothing and to espouse white wealth was at the cornerstone of his/her psyche.

My sisters, hear these poetic words, and rid yourselves of assimilation to white beauty:

Black skin girl you are confused, when you look in the mirror your subconscious has programmed your mind and your consciousness to envision, soft fair skin, long silky hair. The mirror that stares back at you and spits at you is your truth, and you are far away from the beauty the magazines and media espouse to you, in that harsh mirror that gazes back at you. Like the beautiful ripple in a long black stream of rejection and pain. So you attack the parameters of your afro hair, with a thick brush, a hot tong that burns your brown skin, you hear the hot breath, and the electric grey noise from the screech of the blow from the dryer that irritates your skin, and you apply wet white cream against your soft unfettered scalp which burns your scalp. You draw the lines of your lips and paste dolphin fat, with red paint against your strawberry full lips; you mask the soft black nutrients of your dark skin, with the harassment of light brown foundation against the pores of your dark skin, slap red and pink blusher against the imagination of red rosy white cheeks. Arm the banks of the River Nile, with black poisonous Mascara around the ropes of your dark brown eyes, you bargain with beauty, and insert against the will of your irritated and sore eyes, the light brown, blue, green or on occasion hazel contact lenses, and apply that contour to that flat African nose.

Black skin girl, you glue on the fake white acrylics of your nails, to hide the stumpy-ness of your fat dark fingers, decorated with the burnt black ashes of eczema. You hear the thoughts of you applying skin bleach, every morning, in a desperate haze to avert the wide eyes of your black skin, to mute the black melanin that stains the vision of beauty that beckons to me. Before, you put on the strains of a wig made from horsehair, designed in the fabric of white women, which is perceived to be perfect silky flowing hair, just so that you and I don't feel ugly and yet, I still do not feel beautiful. So, I buy into the psychology of social class, and slap a designer handbag, against the banks of my hips, designer shoes to stamp my beauty and relevance in your face. For society has taught me that the black woman has been overlooked, she is the least desirable species, so I create my own version of beauty that mirrors the white woman, for she is surely the pinnacle of beauty.

Black skin girl, your subconscious tells you, you are ugly. I can hear your words dry up against the windows of the hot iron mirror, it says: I do not see images of myself in fashion magazines, on posters, models, everything in society paints me as ugly. Even the black boys prefer the white or mix raced girls. What can I do? Daddy was never around to tell me I was pretty, he left my mother for a white woman with green eyes, long silky blonde hair like the golden sands of heaven. She bore mixed-race children for him, with their fair light mulatto skin, and green eyes. So I wear my green contact lenses every day, if only to remind me that I can bear some semblance to their perfection.

My vision of beauty is not the vision of beauty that society and pop culture tells me, but how do I invoke and raise the battered self-esteem of my black skin? My natural black hair that blows against the dark shadows of assimilation in the wind. Why can't my form of beauty, be beauty too? Why is assimilation to the white codes of racial beauty, the only beauty that must exist, can nobody help us black-skinned girls? My identity is subdued by a racial code, which pits black skin girls at the bottom of the beauty hierarchy. Because they fear the power of black beauty, when it is unbroken. You see the mirror they have created for us black skin girls to look in, is a lie. Our minds are tricked to hate and mutilate ourselves and aspire to be the white woman.

But black skin girls, we must be strong and try to love ourselves, you see pop beauty steals elements of our fashion when it suits them, our full lips, our hips, our bums, when we all know at a certain time, we were called ugly, fat and unsightly because of this. We must as black skin girls unite in our unaltered beauty, creating our own fashion, our own idealisation of beauty and our own magazines, which promote black beauty. For it is only within this path that the mirror that causes us to attack the black nutrients of our unaltered black beauty, will be broken. You see black skin girls, we have been hypnotised into assimilation to the white woman, yet the white woman wants to be us, and so we as black skin girls must resign from the subconscious mirror that has programmed our minds and visions of ourselves as ugly and unworthy.

Listen to me carefully my brothers and sisters, the fabricated Neo-Colonial Mirror that white Hollywood has slowly etched into the minds of humanity. That is, the creation of this archetypal white beauty that sits so frivolously at the top of the blood-soaked racial pyramid, looking down, smiling at all other black forms of beauty from this earthly realm, has kept the black race trapped in a hypnotic circular prism of mental inferior enslavement.

If you look around, your idealisation as a black person is informed by white colonial propaganda via its IT hegemony (i.e. reflections of beauty, through Movies, TV programs and images such as Baywatch, the Beauty and the Beast, Pocahontas, images of Jesus Christ with white skin, and long silky hair when he was, in fact, a Jew, action heroes etc.). These fragments will impact your concept of power, authority, right and wrong, even beauty. For example, African features of a flat nose, afro hair, dark skin, within the psychological programming of the Neo-Colonial Hollywood Mirror, is perceived to be less attractive.

The recurrent and subconscious theme that tie white beauty at the top of the racial hierarchy is the Neo-Colonial Hollywood idealisation of the white person as pure, the saviour, perfection, white love, and idealisations that when constantly viewed and watched on TV's, heard on radios and cinemas globally. This begins to become internalised and consequently permeates your mind, your psychological vision and identity. It's a very simple question, why is the black beauty industry enriching so many white men? Because black women's idealisation of beauty stems from the Neo-Colonial Hollywood Mirror, namely: long silky hair (weave and wigs), fairer skin (skin bleaching creams), and a pointier nose, like that of a white woman.

Black women, I say in jubilation, celebrate your afro hair, do not choose to wear a weave or wig simply to assimilate to white beauty, because your conceptualisation of beauty is mired and blinded by the Neo-Colonial Hollywood Mirror. Instead, celebrate your dark skin, your flat nose, thick hair, and your curvaceous bodies, celebrate your mother tongue. Why do blacks use the terms sisters and brothers, aunties and uncles for familiarity? It derives from the reductionism of all elements that humanity has to offer after one is enslaved, raped, rebranded and divorced from the umbilical cord by force, all that is left in a foreign land is a bond, so yes, my brothers and sisters you are my family, our heritage bound by blood, hardship and the recreational power of pain.

How unwise are we black people, to be ensnared and seduced by Hollywood's Neo-Colonial Mirror in current times, like the blood isn't still wet from our ancestor's enslavement? Was it not long ago that our thick lips were frowned upon that our black women's curvaceous bodies were referred to as unsightly and savage, for which white fashion designers created corsets to tame? For example, in the 19th-Century Saartjie Baartman[xxii] a black woman from South Africa's Eastern Cape was brought to Europe on false pretences by a British doctor, stage-named the "Hottentot Venus" was exhibited around "freak shows" in London and Paris, with crowds invited to look at her "big buttocks". Baartman has become a symbol of the degradation and subjugation experienced by the Khoisan tribe and black women.

Her brain, skeleton and sexual organs remained on display in a Paris museum until 1974. When, the South African government[xxiii] negotiated the repatriation of her remains, where she was not buried until 2002. Baartman's body has reflected the negative global perception around the black female physique.

Now, White Hollywood through its Neo-Colonial Hollywood Mirror has decided that elements of black beauty: thick lips, curvaceous hips is now beauty? The masses by the millions fuel the tables of plastic surgeons to steal elements of our black identity that suit them at their discretion, let us please create our independent black identities free from white encroachment.

The white man's psychological Neo-Colonial Hollywood Mirror chains, not only controls how black men look at themselves but our black identities, remember our identity is not only linked to our self-determination but also how we view righteousness and beauty, not just internally but externally and also psychologically. Relatedly, the inkling of love that is the relationship between a black man and woman, namely, the identity of Black love, becomes conceptually and psychologically mired in agony. As the identity of such love created in the Neo-Colonial Hollywood Mirror is born out of pain and struggle, which again encourages assimilatory aspirations to white relationships and white forms of love displayed in movies and TV. In comparison to the idealisation of universal, free, Disney, white love, which is in opposition to nothing.

Simply put, love is the identity of beauty without conditions and chains, if this Neo-Colonial Hollywood Mirror that reflects our black identity is sewn into a clear pre-existing racial hierarchy (i.e. the Neo-Colonial Hollywood Mirror) how can we freely love ourselves and show love to our black women and children, and in turn how do our women love and respect us? If we do not know who we are looking at in this Neo-Colonial Hollywood Mirror that increasingly defines our black identity. We shamelessly buy into the ideology of Black Hollywood (i.e. the black elite, the black celebrity or actor, athlete or musical artist) a phenomenon created by the white man. Admission to this language enslaves us psychologically, this assimilatory rhetoric is another idealisation developed in the Neo-Colonial Hollywood Mirror, which instantly places the black man inside the racial pyramid as an inferior species at the bottom. Within which, it voices the colonial narrative and assimilation to white Hollywood.

Subsequently, faint hierarchical parallels are drawn by the Neo-Colonial Hollywood Mirror between white Hollywood, which creates black Hollywood as an assimilating other, who like the little inferior brother is still in pursuit of his big brother's white dream. In this colonial vapour, on the one hand, the success of the black elite is attributed to black entertainers. On the other hand, within this colonial vapour, black lawyers, bankers, entrepreneurs, doctors or business owners become less desirable. Note that when the black individual is spoken off in Western human society, he is almost always associated or pinned against an imagined: idea, pursuit, an image, a characteristic, a physical feature that has been socialised by the white man in order to cage and draw subconscious bias against the black man. By creating these measures and inhibiting criteria's when the global community imagines the word black, the white man can create, control and manipulate the psychological being of what the black man is. Which in turn permeates into reality, and erodes the black man's ontological existence.

Following on, it begs the question why has there been an increase in interracial relationships? Is this because of globalisation? Or the idealisation by the black man or black woman of the white partner as superior in their minds? Or is it the rebelliousness and attention garnered by a white woman, who seeks to defy stereotypical idealisations of a white male partner, by dating a black man? Or the colonial mirror that has reflected the black man as animals, savage beasts, linking our sex to bestiality, the porn industry with its Neo-Colonial Hollywood Mirror projecting us black men as being better lovers, having larger genitals, a fetish to be explored? Or is it an insecure white woman who against her equal the "white man" feels insecure and unjustified, she seeks to be superior in a relationship because she suffers from a lack of self-esteem, therefore she dates a black man to feel like his colonial Massa?

Going further, she may even be committing an "internal" good by dating a race typified in the colonial mirror as below her, subconsciously tying her psychological righteous white hegemon complex to that of the white person giving aid to black African children, which she stamps all over her social media. Or adopting a black African child, as an onslaught of Hollywood actors did like it was a fashion statement. Or similarly, feeding starving children in Africa?

Some black men wonder why their white wives or girlfriends consistently stare at other black men desirably, or why they consistently date a string of black men, and only black men. They rather use the term: I like black men, rather than I like you. Or I love black skin, rather than I love your personality. One ponders, is it because you are a black object to be sexually experienced, to be tempered with and tried? Is it because you are not seen or wanted for your consciousness, her white psyche that has been seduced by the Neo-Colonial Hollywood Mirror, ensures she latches onto the continual curiosity and sexual experimentations of the imagined exotic black man. Or does she simply love one for who they are regardless of colour? Or is this Lion of Judah's way of getting the white man to accept the black man, which he has worked so hard to subjugate and recreate as his subordinate. I will let you decide.

The Deception of the Neo-Colonial Hollywood Mirror

Over centuries of racial engineering, within the art of identity deconstruction, the white man developed Hollywood's Neo-Colonial Mirror as a global ontological projection of its psychological power. This mirror allows the white man to program the global community's minds, the ability to control the mind, and feelings and concepts of morality, provide a level of power and control, which has never before been seen in humanity's history. This is what makes the white man's reign of hegemony so unique, in current modern times. The white man, although possessing a history as violent colonisers, convince the world that they are on a crusade of spreading civilsation and morality. Eventually emerging as the world's policeman, by teaching the human mind how to judge and classify, how to treat people who look different from them. This allows the white man to uphold his fabricated "righteousness". To enforce his visions, his forced realities as the righteous protector, the morally superior white being, the ironic preserver of peace. Even though, every major modern-day conflict that is ongoing is either directly or indirectly related to causality that the white man has created, in his conquest to control and destroy identities.

This extensive poisonous psychological white industrial complex with its development of white supremacy is like the blinding black prism of a subconscious vapour, which is so powerful it controls our minds, our hopes, it controls our relationships, in this way it controls our identities. Which like the beautiful dark yellow sun has refracted itself and cast shadows across all ethnic minorities of this world, placing the black man at the bottom of the racial pyramid, with the white man at the top. Remember, the so-called American dream that pits black men and women at the bottom of the racial pyramid is the facet of the white man's Neo-Colonial Hollywood Mirror that he has created, it is the white man's distorted dream for you his perceived subject.

Moreover, he subsequently, imposes the white man's laws which afford the white race, "white privilege" with lesser prison sentences for similar crimes committed by white people, that which black men disproportionally receive longer prison sentences and even death for the same crimes. For example, African-Americans have a higher probability than white Americans to be arrested; once arrested, they are more likely to be convicted; and once convicted, and they have a higher probability of receiving longer prison sentences. African-American adults are 5.9 times more likely to be incarcerated than whites and Hispanics[xxiv]. As of 2001, one of every three black boys born in that year, had the potential to go to prison in his lifetime, as could one of every six Latinos, versus one of every seventeen white boys[xxv].

If we look historically at the 1640s, John Punch, a black servant, escaped bondage with two white servants. Once the black servant was caught, the two white servants received additional years of servant duties, while punch the black servant, was enslaved for life as punishment. In the wake of Bacon's Rebellion, in which free and enslaved black people aligned themselves with poor white people against the US government. Laws to curb such defiance against white bourgeoisie governance and order, meant black people in America were being enslaved for life, while the protections of whiteness were formalised to protect white "lower classes" from such harsh punishment. It is clear here even looking historically that, the white man and black man will never be equal, even to this day such white privilege is still being dished out to the white race. This is due to the fact that the Neo-Colonial Hollywood Mirror has conditioned the white psyche, from generation to generation, whereby the white man sees a black slave to be imprisoned for life, not a protester against injustice.

By creating and perpetuating policies that allow for such racial disparities to exist in the criminal justice system, the United States is in violation of its obligations under Article 2 and Article 26 of the International Covenant on Civil and Political Rights to ensure that all its citizens, regardless of race are treated equally under the law.

We see this inbred colonial psychology present in current times. For instance, in 2016, black Americans comprised 27% of all individuals arrested in the United States, this is double the share of the total population[xxvi]. Black youth accounted for 15% of all U.S. children, yet made up 35% of juvenile arrests in that year[xxvii]. White Americans overlook the fact that "people of colour" are disproportionately victims of crime and discount the prevalence of this prejudice in the criminal justice system[xxviii]. And importantly within their psychologies.

The white man in his psyche does not attribute human characteristics to black people, his innate psychological objective is the preservation of his neo-colonial hegemony. Black self-determination is in opposition to the seat of the white man's power. That being, his profound ability to divide and rule through identity eradication. Understand, to divide is to create the other as something different, to rule is to create a demarcation that sets you as superior to that other. Simply put, the white psyche has convinced itself and enforced social, legal, economic, academic, political and military campaigns to reinforce the fabrications of its white righteous hegemony.

Re-establishing black consciousness is key to understanding the truth of black identity distortion; the white man has been able to eradicate black consciousness through manipulating and destroying our black identities. Our consciousness is part of what forms the self, our psyche informs our state of awareness, yet our awareness has been muted by the powerful reflections of the paralysing Neo-Colonial Hollywood Mirror. My brothers understand, the white man's fears the black race united because the white man fears the black man's potential to lead.

In this current day, the viral pandemic humanity has been facing since 2019. We see how racialised psychology and the Neo-Colonial Hollywood Mirror through the media have created biological racism. With media headlines, arguing that black people are more at risk from the deadly virus, with other headlines stating that black people are not immune. Given that a third of all unwell COVID-19 patients, in the United Kingdom are from Black and Minority Ethnic backgrounds, according to new data. From the 2,249 critical patients registered in the UK, up until April 3rd 2020, 13.8 percent were recorded as "Asian", 13.6 percent as "Black" and 6.6 percent as "Other", based on reports from the Intensive Care National Audit and Research Centre (ICNARC).

What underpins these narratives is that ethnic minorities are an inferior race; white people should avoid interaction with minorities, given that they are more prone to the deadly Coronavirus. What emerges is biological racism, white psychology doesn't take into account that ethnic minorities are vastly underrepresented in health research, and there is a lack of access to healthcare, there is lower quality care given higher poverty levels within Ethnic minority concentrated areas. Omar Khan, the director of Runnymede Trust, argues: "There's a biological racism in this kind of assuming that ethnic minorities are inherently more likely to have diabetes, even things like heart disease and diabetes have social and economic determinants – things like diet, exercise, discrimination and poverty."

Similarly, Salman Waqar, general secretary of the British Islamic Medical Association, said: "BAME patients are vastly under-represented in health research and there many things we simply do not know. Urgent action is needed to understand why they may be experiencing this disease burden from COVID-19 and take appropriate action to prevent further deaths." [xxix]

The power of the Neo-Colonial Hollywood Mirror in relation to COVID-19 media headlines, conditions the human psyche such that we do not acknowledge the health inequalities between white and black people. Namely, a lack of research on ethnic minorities, factors such as wealth disparities, poverty, over-crowding in homes/areas, and occupational structure (i.e. having the ability to work from home or not) which limits human interactions. Are factors that contribute to the degrees of viral exposure a racial group has, and consequently how widespread the infections become. African-Americans face a higher threat of exposure to the virus, largely given that in terms of structural healthcare prevention techniques, just 20% of black workers reported being entitled to work from home, compared with about 30% of their white counterparts, according to the Economic Policy Institute[xxx].

If we look back historically and look at major health pandemics, over the last few centuries, for example: the plague 1720, Cholera 1820, Spanish flu 1920 and the Coronavirus 2020. Ethnic minorities were heavily exposed to such pandemics given structural health inequalities and living conditions.

Wasim Hanif, a professor at the University Hospital Birmingham and a trustee of the South Asian Health Foundation UK, noted: "We need to ask for more ethnicity data so that we know a little more about these patients; whether these are younger patients, what their underlying conditions are, and what the other factors are. That is what needs to be looked into."

"The reality is nobody is immune from the health and economic impacts from COVID-19. But existing structural inequalities mean that impoverished ethnicities, will experience higher exposure to COVID-19 more than others," said Zubaida Haque, deputy director of the race equality think tank Runnymede Trust. "BME groups in the UK are amongst the poorest of socioeconomic groups. There are extremely high rates of child poverty and they're much more likely to be employed in low-paid, precarious work. They're also much more likely to be living in multigenerational households, which make BME elderly people more at risk of severe illness from COVID-19. BME women are particularly vulnerable as they are more likely to be in precarious work than their white counterparts," she added.

A 2017 report by the Joseph Rowntree Charitable Trust on race and poverty, found that the UK poverty rate was twice as high for Black Minority communities, in comparison to white communities, this is seen as a driving factor behind the larger spread of the Coronavirus among black identities.

Similarly, the US has experienced racialised media narratives in relation to COVID-19, with racial biological narratives being echoed, reinforcing the injustice of black citizens. This resonates with racial injustices in healthcare, including facility closures and limits on public health insurance plans like Medicaid and Medicare. African-Americans are twice as likely to have no health insurance compared with their white counterparts, and more likely to live in medically underserved areas, where primary care is meagre or too expensive.

Unconscious racial bias can also contribute to unequal health outcomes, especially when health professionals are inexperienced with black patients, according to the Journal of General Internal Medicine. The Century Foundation found that healthcare providers located within the majority of African-American or Latin neighbourhoods tend to provide lower-quality care, the inherent psychology in this is those ethnic minorities are lower down on the racial pyramid, if bad services are rendered nobody will care, the black and latin people will not have the financial means to hold health care professionals accountable if malpractice takes place. In fact, their lack of awareness and lower education level means they will not be able to tell the difference. This is the inherent racial bias that exists in the psyche of the Westernised health caregiver, which is driven by the Neo-Colonial Hollywood Mirror.

This is reinforced by the CEO of Advancing Health Equity, who inferred that government responses can be racialised. For example, she noted that as the virus first spread, the US Centres for Disease Control and Prevention, only released and prioritised testing guidelines for those who had travelled abroad. That meant Blackstock's mostly black patients in low-income areas of Brooklyn and Queens were not tested as rapidly, as their white patients in Manhattan who had the financial means to travel were the priority[xxxi].

For example, around 70% of Coronavirus deaths in Louisiana are African-Americans, and the Covid-19 deaths in New Orleans, 60% of the population that make up these deaths were black Americans. Detroit, which is almost 80% black, has the most concentrated Coronavirus cases in the state of Michigan. The death rate in the city accounts for 40% of overall deaths in the state.

In Chicago, which is 30% black, black Americans account for 70% of all Coronavirus cases in the city. "We know all too well that there are general disparities in health outcomes that play along racial lines and the same may be true for this virus," said Ngozi Esike, director of the Illinois department of public health.

In the same fashion, in China, black African students and workers are being discriminated against, as COVID-19 carriers, given their subconscious perspective of inferior dirty black skin. Here we can see how the power of the Neo-Colonial Hollywood Mirror, has conditioned all other ethnicities of colour, into perceiving black people as the dirtiest and lowest on the racial pyramid. And likely carriers and spreaders of the deadly Corona disease, therefore hotels are refusing to accept them, they are being thrown out of their apartments, and are involuntarily being quarantined by the police. When in fact, the Coronavirus reportedly originated in Wuhan, China. It is shocking to see how powerful, the racial psychological conditioning of the mind is, and how this can impact our relations with other people, who are also ethnic minorities.

Now inbred in this racist biology is the subconscious reflection of the Neo-Colonial Hollywood Mirror. For instance, if we look historically during the 18th century during the yellow fever outbreak in the Americas, much of the ideas about black people correlate to current day racist biological perceptions now espoused. In the 1740s, yellow fever spread through cities such as Charleston, South Carolina, driving people into hallucination, vomiting, bleeding, and causing widespread death. The physician, John Lining, made notes about the disease after inspecting slave ships and their consignment in Charleston. His conclusion was that white people were catching the disease, and black people were immune. These observations helped reinforce colonial based ideas that Black Africans had supernatural immunisation to some of the deadliest diseases in the Americas[xxxii].

Lining's notes became the blueprint for a physician, Dr Benjamin Rush, thus in 1793 when a yellow fever outbreak spread through Philadelphia, Pennsylvania. Nearly, half of the population fled to Philadelphia in that period, while many African-Americans stayed in the city at the bid of Rush, who wanted to train them to nurse, care-take, and dig graves for the thousands of white people dying of yellow fever. Rush's innate psychological belief was that black people were immune from the disease, and black Philadelphians believed him when he told them that they were immune. It is interesting how the black mind, does not challenge the "truths", that the white voice espouses, or rather, the black man is entrapped in his slave mentality, to never challenge Massa.

The white man told them that it was their Christian duty to help care for the lives of white Philadelphians. However, Rush was wrong in his psychological assertion about black people. Many of the African-Americans in his medical group contracted yellow fever, hundreds of them died. The Philadelphia massacre of black people is evidence of the long-running colonial narrative about black identities and deadly diseases.

As Dr Rana Hogarth wrote in her piece, Medicalizing Blackness, about the 1793 yellow fever pandemic in Philadelphia: "The idea of innate black immunity placed an undue burden on the city's black inhabitants. For those black people who did stay behind to help, it meant buying into a belief that at its core defined their bodies as being distinctive and unequal to whites."

Such current-day ideologies spread across social media, whether made literally or comically, condition the psyche of the global community, and put black people in harm's way. This psychological conditioning is rooted in racist beliefs that hark back to the 18th-century yellow fever epidemic that killed many blacks.

Medical theories about black disease immunity persisted after the Philadelphia yellow fever pandemic and were used politically and economically to justify the enslavement of Africans, to help enrich the white man. Some medical authorities went further, adding that this black immunity power was linked not just to racial biology, but to certain geographic locations and climates. These perspectives ended up as part of the Confederate South's arguments for preserving its plantation and slave-based economy.

The climate theory suggested that particular deadly diseases, couldn't survive in warmer temperatures. Interestingly, in present times this same line of thinking was used by a cruise ship line about the Coronavirus, to persuade people to keep booking trips with them. As the Miami New Times reported on March 10th 2020, Norwegian Cruises ordered sales workers to give customers scripted lines such as: "The Coronavirus can only survive in cold temperatures, so the Caribbean is a fantastic choice for your next cruise," and, "Scientists and medical professionals have confirmed that the warm weather of the spring will be the end of the Coronavirus."

We must acknowledge that there is no scientific evidence, which suggests that the Coronavirus is weakened at any temperature, just like the claims of earlier centuries that diseases like yellow fever can't survive in tropical conditions.

We recently witnessed leading French doctor Jean-Paul Mira the head of intensive care at Cochin hospital in Paris, arguing racistly during a debate on TV, saying: "If I can be provocative, shouldn't we be doing this study in Africa, where there are no masks, no treatments, and no resuscitation?"

"A bit like as it is done elsewhere for some studies on Aids. In prostitutes, we try things because we know that they are highly exposed and that they do not protect themselves."

Similarly, we can see historically that such racist ideology has not changed, in the 18th century among white medical professionals, they believed that black skin was thicker than white skin, which emboldened doctors to experiment on black bodies. One major medical idea was that black people feel less pain and suffering than other races, an idea that became the foundation for the surgical experimentations that Dr James Marion Sims performed on black women in his quest to perfect procedures for fixing reproductive problems. Today he is considered the "father of gynaecology." We can see here how the power of the Neo-Colonial Hollywood Mirror, and its creation of the black specimen, has been destructive to the lives of black people. And how the inherent ideology of black people having supernatural immunity and strength is correlated with that of the animal.

Black identities have been engineered by the white man, to envy each other's identities, particularly black identities whose likeness appears closer to white people. Whether this is in, wealth, status, academia, television, skin complexion, looks, accent, or clothing. Thus, the black man is habitually lost experiencing a prolonged state of an identity crisis, which spawns low self-esteem, self-loafing and afflictions related to rejection and disappointment. So powerful is this affliction, we as black people begin to feel guilty for being black, we even try to anticipate and cater to how our presence might adversely affect the feeling of safety and psyche of white people, who are blinded by the fabricated stereotypical neo-colonial depictions of black people.

Understand, the white man with his control of the media, and his Information Technology hegemony has blinded and stifled basic human integrity, by continuing the psychosis of black identity eradication. Uncle Sam is indeed an IT hegemon; it is another form of power more dangerous than hypersonic missiles and more dangerous than nuclear weapons. It is the ability to construct a false reality, based on the domineering power of the media's neo-colonial voice, which heavily informs our subconscious, our truths, our perceptions, our identities, and consequently our black self-determination.

Responsibility of the Created Black "Elite" and Black Self-Determination

The earliest memory I have of a black role model was a slew of black rappers, footballers, basketball players, boxers and Rhythm and Blues singers. There was no idealisation of a professor, banker, writer, entrepreneur, scientist, lawyer, artist, IT programmer, architect, designer, doctor or politician, within the projection of the Neo-Colonial Hollywood Mirror upon my black psyche. Therefore, this programming of my mind meant that the creation of the 'black elite' by the white man, had become synonymous with the existence of Black male celebrities/entertainers. Similarly, those who went on to become African statesmen, had usually gone to Western boarding schools and Universities. In my view, black celebrities have a social responsibility, given the platform and elevation that the Neo-Colonial Hollywood Mirror provides for them.

In the current day racist environment in which, black male genocide is being committed by the white man. I wonder, when black celebrities have the world listening to them, whether that be through music, television, radio, sports, what message are they conveying and how is it aiding black self-determination? When black genocide is happening in the most cunning of ways, and its core focus is to eradicate black consciousness in the haze of white assimilatory hymns.

My point is, there is a lack of successful male black role models, given the profound ability of the white man to mentally and physically break the black man in this Neo-Colonial Hollywood Mirror. Rappers, athletes are the positive white idealisation that is reflected onto the masses of many black youths via the Neo-Colonial Hollywood Mirrors. Black celebrities become the black elite, according to the white man's depiction of the imagined black self and white assimilatory success.

In this way, my view is that black celebrities have a responsibility to reflect black self-determination and a renewed black identity on their media platforms to black youths. Instead of falling into the trap of the Neo-Colonial Hollywood Mirror by refracting vanity (e.g. cars, watches, private jets, yachts and cash), this is the white man's assimilatory dream for us, who seeks to hold us in chains at the bottom of the racial pyramid. For example, when a rapper gets a record deal and is given a financial advance which is paramount to debt, there have been instances where they have spent this money on buying gold chains or diamonds necklaces. One asks why a gold chain? Why diamonds on their teeth and watches? Why is it that this is the first thing a black artist from a socially deprived background buys, after receiving a large sum of cash? One ponders, is this a lack of education?

My view is that, it stems from a lack of self-worth and wanting to validate yourself and self-worth through material items because the black man lacks self-value. These black artists aspire to be seen in a society that has rejected and overlooked them, that gold chain or diamond necklace in their black psyche adds value and visibility to their eradicated identities, increasing their status and position on the white man's racial pyramid. For example, why buy jewellery instead of investing in a property you can own and gain equity on, all of these indictments are informed by the Neo-Colonial Hollywood Mirror and the destruction of black identity and a lack of education.

To the extent that a black man is willing to kill another individual for trying to steal this gold or diamond chain, remember this gold chain or diamond chain, is the only identity that informs his self-worth, value and self-esteem. To fleece his chain is to further eradicate his identity, and to take further control from his re-created miniature identity, in a historical environment when the white man has taken all control from the black man. As little as this chain sounds to you, in his psyche this gold chain represents his self-worth and his identity upon the racial pyramid.

The Neo-Colonial Hollywood Mirror offers an alternative to selling drugs and eventually ending up in prison as another slave for us black men, becoming successful in Massa's eyes in the colonial mirror is to become an athlete, rapper, comedian, entertainer or actor. No educational barriers to entry, you become a slave to a white man's organisation selling your body and soul to entertain those who would rather see you die or in chains, this is no joke but sadly a reality.

We as black men need to be refracting self-determination and a spiritual cleansing of the yoke that has been stuck in front of our eyes for so long. We need to build our own economic structures amongst ourselves, instead of being envious of each other and wondering who is going to be closer to being on Massa's next best slave on the Forbes list, this constant pursuit and assimilation to the white man will keep us in chains.

A sad example was watching Donald Trump abuse and exploit black rapper Kanye West, a gifted musician. A man whose identity was lost when his anchor, his mother, who enforced his black self-determination died, a man so blinded by the Neo-Colonial Hollywood Mirror that he had liposuction, a similar procedure that killed his mother because he was so blinded by the negative power of social media and perceptions of his identity, convoluted with insecurity, and the worship of the racial pyramid. It zapped any logical sense from his mind. What man would undergo the same procedure that killed his anchor, his black mother for the sake of vanity? We should not berate this artist but pray for him that the lion of Judah brings back his self-determination and clarity of mind. That the black nutrients and self-determination that his black mother stitched within him spiritually, through her golden umbilical cord, will rediscover its black son.

Kanye West's interview with Donald Trump was a clear example of a slave boy trying desperately to appease his slave master. You see what people don't understand is that, Kanye is striving to co-exist with his "other" the white man, in co-existing he is at least someone rather than nothing in his psyche. Or put differently, the top house nigger or indeed the black man who marries a white woman in order to elevate his perceived status on the neo-colonial racial pyramid.

In this, he wants to be perceived as a king amongst his black tribe, an elite amongst his black peer group, he wants billionaire status as he alluded to; which he feels will bring him greater respect and power amongst white men. He makes references to white men and white identities, Walt Disney, Ralph Lauren and Steve Jobs, which are his idealisations of assimilatory perfection, what the white man psychologically has compelled him to view as success through their colonial mirrors. Like most black men, who seek respect or who aspire to be like the white man and possess things or ideas associated with the white man espoused in this Neo-Colonial Hollywood Mirror.

Consequently, the white man has tried to convince black men that we are the antithesis of any form of fulfilment or success. And he has reinforced this through economic structures to eradicate rebellion. What Kanye West doesn't understand is that he will forever be a black man. The colonial yoke, the Hollywood mirror, has still not been lifted, trying to assimilate to these things will only reinforce the racial pyramid and chains that bound his neck and muzzle his voice. We must create idealisations of a strong and successful black man, which is not pinned against or held against the achievements of a white man, it is only at that point, we will make headway in changing the subconscious prejudice and bias that has informed the black experience in this millennium.

Indeed, we black individuals who look down on other blacks, are hypnotised in the Neo-Colonial Hollywood Mirror and are lost fools. Due to the fact that you have gone to 'elite' schools, prestigious universities, you have attained the means to join elite white clubs, establishments, seats in government, or you lack clarity over social issues. Just realise that if you buy into this Neo-Colonial Hollywood Mirror that you are above your own black brothers, you are buying into the idea of the white man. Who uses the few of one tribe to rule the others, the white man has done this historically by attributing European features to one African tribe and therefore viewing them as superior to other tribes, giving them economic, military goods in order for them to invade, kill, and rule their own neighbours.

The white man has treated all tribes in the global community as inferior species, you can only be bought and sold, ruled and conquered by the white man if you buy into their Neo-Colonial Hollywood Mirror, if you allow yourself to be sold into the idea that you are elite or above your brethren's, when really, we are all just flesh and blood, remember in a police line-up, we are all the same in the white man's psyche, ask OJ Simpson.

Black Mental Enslavement

My brothers, we must wake up from our nocturnal sleep, and acknowledge that our minds have been enslaved, we have no identity as free black men or women, and the white man has robbed our sanity in the most cunning of ways. That is, the subconscious power of assimilation to the white race means that the black man's propensity to act independently and within his consciousness is muted. The black man wants a slice, even if it is a fraction of the white privilege afforded to the white race. When this privilege isn't afforded to him, he feels rejected and seeks to create this racial power structure within his own black racial pyramid with him at the top. Alternatively, he rejects white identity creation and forms the governance of his own black nationalism or he falls prey to the constant pursuit of assimilation to the white man, leaving him insecure. As the foundation of his identity is built on no identity, but rather the pillars of white assimilation.

In the same way, the white man has created, endorsed and socialised psychologically the notion of black-on-black crime, please take a step back, cleanse your mind of the subconscious Neo-Colonial Hollywood Mirrors that has permeated your mind, for one moment, and think about this loaded concept. It makes no logical sense, it is the same effect of saying 1-1= 3, and it is reductionist and empty at its most.

But interestingly, it is one of the biggest tricks the white man through his Neo-Colonial Hollywood Mirror has played on black society and the wider global community. What is most interesting is how authorities, academics and the media have not challenged this concept but subconsciously accepted this colonial narrative as a truth and a norm. The undercurrents of this colonial narrative paint the black man as an uncontrollable animal, prone to illogical violence.

It is interesting that the Neo-Colonial Hollywood Mirror intertwines this concept, with the glamorisation of black gang culture, or in the UK specific police forces set aside (Operation Trident) to control the supposedly uncontrollable black hooligans by necessary genocide, imprisonment and death. By sanctioning such languages in our minds, in politics, in the media, and in universities, my black brothers and sisters we are sanctioning our own deaths. I ask you, when a white youth kills another white youth from the same neighbourhood, does the concept of white-on-white crime exist? Would the white man or the Neo-Colonial Hollywood Mirror reflect and socialise and accept such a notion? Never! As it does not fit into the righteous Neo-Colonial Hollywood Mirror narrative or image. For example, a simple group of young black children standing on a street corner, become imagined as a violent gang to be subdued, a simple group of young white children standing on a street corner become imagined as innocent friends.

I say by logical extension and for us to eradicate the imagined notion of black-on-black crime. In areas of acute deprivation, which is systemic across black communities disproportionately, there is a higher level of crime, where there is crime and no hope, there is alcohol and drug abuse for the escapism of harsh realities, and thereby increased levels of violence, put simply. Survival is a key motif, which drives people not only impoverished blacks but humans within the global community, generally to pursue illegal means to be able to put food on the table and feed their families. The pursuit of living the life of luxury that the Neo-Colonial Hollywood Mirror creates is a form of entrapment, and a clear path to imprisonment for those without the means to legitimately enjoy luxuries espoused by the elite white social classes.

Importantly, and linked to the Neo-Colonial Hollywood Mirror, is the glamorisation of gang culture and violence. This glamorisation creates an academy of destruction, whereby the young black male is called to assimilate to a sub-gang culture that has been created by the white man, through the media. A false form of respect and power is developed because of the Neo-Colonial Hollywood Mirrors subconscious voice. Given white society overlooks and silences the black boy from his youth, he seeks respect and acceptance elsewhere, a new identity. The black boy is not even aware that the white man has created this gang identity, for him to be destroyed. The interesting thing about this form of assimilation to black gang culture is that there is a real awareness of the steps that a black individual takes to join a gang, however, there isn't an awareness of why they do. Similar to the subconscious voice of assimilation, that the Neo-Colonial Hollywood Mirror calls upon, in order for the global community to adhere to white superiority.

Similar to the Ku Klux Klan, hatred becomes the driving force behind the gang, for example, developing a secret hand code or handshake, a particular way to speak, and a particular way to wear their bandana's/masks. Only so the black boy can turn around and shoot another black boy a few blocks down the road, and he is fundamentally unaware of why he is doing it. Being accepted is his objective and gaining respect with his new family – the gang – and the identity the gang provides for him, becomes his obsession.

This gang assimilation uses black voices to call other blacks, by this I mean older black gang members recruiting younger black gang members to "put in work" whether that be through selling drugs, committing robberies or shooting gang rivals, all so that his standing within the gang increases. This bears resemblance to black slaves who would help to catch other slaves, whether that be from the shores of Africa, or runaway slaves on plantation fields in the Americas.

In this, we can see the Neo-Colonial Hollywood Mirror has layers to its voice, and by voice, I mean the ability of this mirror to convey subconscious messages and impart identities on particular ethnicities. For example, it has the ability to focus particularly on black men. Very similar to the art of marketing, and creating and selling to your target market audiences.

This sub-culture for black men is the assimilation to a "gangster's life" the adherence particularly in black gangs of going to jail, drive-by shootings/stabbings, dying, becomes a norm. Which results in high levels of black male incarceration and black deaths by law enforcement officers, which is the aim of the Neo-Colonial Hollywood Mirror. The power of this gang assimilation is so powerful, and is exported internationally through the Neo-Colonial Hollywood Mirror that you see replica gangs within black communities overseas, (e.g. in the UK and France). For example, the black American gangs the Bloods and Crips, who respectively use red and blue bandanas to represent their gangs have replica gangs in the UK, who carry out similar crimes. In fact, the majority of black gangs in the UK now associate their gangs with bandana colours, similar to US gangs. We, as black men, internationally fall into the trap, of identity creation, because we do not have the strength and an awareness of who we are, we are constantly in pursuit of an identity created for us.

In my view, in most cases, Western society breaks the black boy before he becomes the black man, his identity painted by the Neo-Colonial Hollywood Mirror, his harsh treatment by the white man misunderstood, he is antagonised by different idealisations of who and what he should be. On the one hand, negative hysteria from his black brethren, "you are acting white they say," when he speaks formal English rather than "black slang", "you dress like a white boy" when he wears particular clothing not deemed black enough, "he is doing the wrong thing when he goes to school." On the other hand, the Neo-Colonial Hollywood Mirror promotes black gang violence, and drug dealing as a necessary extension and logical component of the black man's identity. Remember, in order for the "other" to destroy your identity, they need to create the parameters to define you, we should not follow our black brethren in these instances as they are blinded by the Neo-Colonial Hollywood Mirror, which sets out the supposed parameters of the black man, a simple trap.

Black Humidity and the White Martyr

My black brothers, let the philosophy of these lines and the identity brought forth, be your self-determination and recreated identities: "you are a chosen people, a royal priesthood, a holy nation, God's special possession that you may declare the praises of him who called you out of darkness into his wonderful light."[xxxiii]

The blinding power of racism is so destructive and frightening, it is subconsciously embedded in judges' minds and the psychologies of those who pass tougher sentences on black men because they are not viewed as human beings, but rather dangerous animals to be locked away and tamed.

Similarly, this is reflected in the lack of media coverage for missing black girls, versus the mass media coverage garnered for missing white girls. Effectively, white women harness privileged roles as violent crime victims in the Western media, this form of racial hierarchy is psychologically implanted and intertwined with white superior cultural imagery of the Western media. For example, black children accounted for 35% of missing children cases in the FBI's database, yet they amounted to only 7% of media references[xxxiv]. This was underpinned by the story of Jayme Closs, the 13-year-old white Wisconsin girl who was kidnapped after her parents were killed, which made national news.

This is juxtaposed to the story of Arianna Fitts, a black 2-year-old child, who went missing in 2016 before her mother was found brutally murdered in the San Francisco Bay Area. Both of these cases are gripping, however, both cases didn't receive the same amount of media attention. These issues are underpinned by the racial hierarchical dichotomy that the Neo-Colonial Hollywood Mirror projects onto the psyche of the white society. This sentiment was echoed by Seong-Jae Min and John C. Feaster, who found that whilst ethnic minorities were disproportionately represented in news coverage, African-American missing children in particular "were significantly underrepresented when compared to national statistics."[xxxv] Similarly, given the power of the Neo-Colonial Hollywood Mirror, and the dehumanisation of black skinned women, and therefore a lack of care shown, black women have an increased risk of dying in pregnancy and miscarriage, as noted by Tommy's National Centre for Miscarriage Research deputy director Professor Siobhan Quenby, from the University of Warwick.

Additionally, during the crack epidemic within black communities in the '70s and '80s particularly in America, the Western media showed no sympathy or care towards such epidemics because it largely afflicted black communities, now that the onset of the opiate epidemic is destroying the fabric of white communities, the US Neo-Colonial Hollywood Mirrors refer to it as a national emergency. Parallels can be drawn with the UK Neo-Colonial Hollywood Mirrors, when the knife crime epidemic largely affected black communities, there was no concern or empathetic media coverage, as it was termed black on black crime. However, when it afflicted white communities, it was referred to as a national crisis to be tackled by the government.

It is clear that the Neo-Colonial Hollywood Mirror is an engine of Anglo-American white supremacy. It is reinforced through the Neo-Colonial Hollywood media with social media, depicting black men as animals, savages, brutes, a sub-human to be treated like animals, and it goes further than just giving us barbaric physical attributes, but it creates stereotypical characteristics, "the angry black man, the angry black woman, why do black women have attitudes they ask? She should be lucky to be in this country, in this workplace, a part of this welfare system, he is playing the race card, all lives matter, not just black lives."

Inherent in all these stereotypical characteristics the white man has created, he reduces black suffering to a simple excuse or schism, he circumvents his blatant racism by creating a martyr out of the white man, having to deal with black repetitive excuses. The white man blinded in his white superior syndrome, will ask show me the evidence of racism? I have seen no evidence of racism they will utter, they will dissect, diminish and pick apart your claim of racism, as though you were ludicrous for raising it. As though the experience of racism was an objective posteriori mathematical formula, which needs to be tested to see if the criteria and benchmark of racism have been met. Note that, it is always a criterion, which the white man wants to see, so they can control, create and change the parameters of your claim of racism, to dismiss your claims completely.

The white man in his racist disease is blinded by his white righteous belief that you are inferior, he genuinely wonders why you are even complaining about not being treated the same way as your white counterparts, as this is the norm, just accept it. At times, the white man will exercise indirect racism,[xxxvi] and micro-aggressions this is not overt racism, but introvert racism. This is treating somebody differently or depriving them of the same opportunities because of the colour of their skin. This is subconscious racism, drawing a psychological racial asymmetry between the same actions a white and black person takes. By this I mean, the white individual, exacts harsher responses to actions that the black individual has undertaken, even though the white individual has done the exact same thing, but receives a less severe response. This prejudice is driven by their skin colour, and the need for the white man to enforce their racial superiority (i.e. it is okay for us to do it because we are white, but you can't do that when you're black).

This is fundamental because psychologically, their minds have been programmed to believe the black race has no voice: so who are you to even complain, you have no right, is what dwells in the prognosis of their white minds. The disease of the superior white syndrome is an infectious virus, so much so that their white consciousness is not even aware of their racist behaviour, but their subconscious is aware of their racism, but they are hypnotised by their white racial imperial right to exercise racism. You see, for the white race, to acknowledge any form of racism is to put their own "white privilege" and defence of "white martyrdom" at severe risk, so their subconscious has programmed their minds to uphold the racist status quo, for the status quo is white supremacy.

Weaved into this, white martyrdom is the subconscious ideology that the black man should accept the Neo-Colonial

Hollywood Mirror and the racial pyramid. Effectively, you as black people are treated sub-humanely, but you must accept this as reality because truly you should be our slave picking cotton. As forbidding as these indictments sound, it is the reality within which we black men walk around in society, within which we go to work, within which we get stopped and searched and antagonised by police officer's, effectively Massa's slave catchers.

It is so psychologically powerful that when we walk into supermarket stores, security guards follow us, even our own black security guards follow us in anticipation of a crime, which has been conceived and fabricated in that individual's mind, their subconscious psyche. Similarily, as a black person sometimes when you speak, the white shop assistant who is serving you, will act like they can't hear you when you speak, therefore you need to repeat yourself or speak louder, these micro-aggressions, are there to let you know we as white people don't want to hear your voice, it is a form of bullying, when this is done repeatedly over years it can become frustrustating and tiring for black people, resulting in the development of hardness to protect ones sensititivies, like a cocoon shell, because everything, even the simplest of things becomes a fight or an issue, even if it's a white shop assistant refusing to hear your order for a coffee.

This stems from the Neo-Colonial Hollywood Mirror, just from merely seeing black skin flash before one's eyes, it sends a subconscious trigger, increased blood flow to arteries like a wild panther has just walked into the store, so powerful is the Neo-Colonial Hollywood narrative it has crept into our subconscious and physically manifested itself as a Rubik facet of heightened fear, and insatiable curiosity about the other – the black man.

I remember the musty cold grey wet London days when I would walk into work, and every day my white boss would look at me like some kind of rare animal, who had just walked into the room. So fascinated was he with my black skin that he forgot I had a name, a personality, a sense of humour, and feelings, he simply could not get over my black skin. It was interesting because the whole team would look at me as though I was about to commit some kind of robbery or offence, so they watched me closely, every minute, every second, every day. They made subconscious notes on what I ate, when I ate, when I went to the toilet, how long I would spend on my lunch breaks. I sometimes wondered what was the difference between myself and a slave on a plantation in Georgia, although I was not physically whipped, the emotional pain of being excluded, being looked at as though I was a criminal, being underpaid, being treated harshly, being perceived as a lady's man for no reason at all apart from the sexualisation of the black man by the media was a damage enough.

With myself and another black colleague, it was an unwritten rule that we would not be seen going to lunch together, talking too much together. As we knew in the white man's psyche, he would imagine a gang and think we were not team players, we were alienating ourselves, and consequently, we would be punished. When the same two white boys in our team went to lunch together consistently, there were no qualms or comments. Fundamentally, it became clear to me that white people fear black people united, they feel a sense of loss of control because their identities are contingent on the ability to divide the other. Interestingly, when I looked back at the Stono Rebellion of 1739, which was the largest slave uprising of the mainland British colonies. Between 60 and 100 black slaves were involved in the rebellion; about 40 black people and 20 white people were killed, other liberation fighters were captured. The response by White lawmakers in South Carolina, fearful of further rebellions was to pass the Negro Act of 1740, which criminalised the assembly, education and moving among the enslaved blacks[xxxvii]. This institutionalised and eliminated the ability of the black slaves to congregate. This legislation has morphed into a subconscious reality for white people, due to centuries of conditioning and massaging this idea into white minds, the white race begins to fear the black race congregated, together and united in any form. Similarly, during the 1831 Nat turner revolt in Southampton County, the Virginia inhabitant, Eleanor Weaver asserted in a letter to family members: "We hope our government will take some steps to put down Negro preaching. It is those large assemblies of Negroes that causes the mischief."

Essentially, the glaring question becomes, why would you even care if two people from the same nationalities go to lunch together? It is subconsciously because the white man feels he has control over you. After all, you are in his psyche his black slave.

The white man sometimes and willingly antagonises black men, similar to a black animal being poked to see its reactions, to see if Massa's textbook on black men would yield likely neo-colonial statistical reports, espoused about the invented, angry black man theorem. A similar experience can be had on a packed train, the sight of a black individual boarding the train can cause a frenzy and a desperate clutch for the handbag, averted eyes, in anticipation of an imagined violent crime that has yet to take place.

Finally, simply just walking down a street of a busy road with white commuters. Interestingly, given the imagined hype and fear of the black man, you would presume that the white individual would step aside to avoid a clash, yet they walk straight into the black person, expecting them to give way. Remember, in the white idealisation the black individual is at the bottom of the racial pyramid, in their psyche you are the slave, not to get in the way of the superior white master, in fact, you should be scuffling away, this colonial subconscious prism is so powerful it has become the underlying cornerstone of the white psyche. Comparatively, this same example can be seen with a white passenger, who believes that they have a rite of passage while driving a car on a road; the black individual driving a car on the same two-way street like a good field nigger should give way for Massa.

The white man sometimes asks and ponders, if the black race is so unhappy living in the US or Europe, why don't they just go back to Africa. Yet, one ponders, if the white man had not raped and plundered my motherland, created international economic systems and supranational organisation that disparaged and disadvantaged African nations, would I even be sitting in this western Society, in their western offices, wearing their western suits, enslaved to Western capitalism. I am a black man, and all the white man can see is my black skin, no matter my economic status, no matter my educational background, I am a black animal to be disciplined in their eyes.

The hypnotic Neo-Colonial Hollywood Mirror made in the white race's image has been a force that has engineered and fostered the subconscious white superior psyche syndrome (i.e. the belief that the white race is superior to all other races, and therefore has the right to impose their will). This has convinced the white race that they have the right to dehumanise, abuse and kill black men, as they look down the racial pyramid with their hegemonic telescope and fabricated righteousness.

It has become the white man's prerogative, subconscious truth, their subconscious bias, their burden to keep the black man in chains, to always remind them that yes: "you are still a slave." At times the white man needs to test their self-conviction, their fabricated hegemonic righteousness, which has given them free rein, as the world's policeman to bomb and kill millions in the global community. The white man antagonises the black man hoping for a violent response to prove the angry black man theorem he created, testing the patience of black men, waiting and expecting us to explode and lose our tempers. In order to justify the need for their continuous wickedness and custodial enslavement of black individuals. Whilst they have alluded themselves to the fact that, if they were given the same treatment, they would lose their tempers also, as common human beings, as part of the global community.

My black men, what I say is, we must exercise righteous patience, refrain from losing our tempers and deny the white man his hegemonic right to exercise his so-called righteous hegemony, for they will enslave you in the prison system, meant to blind, to destroy and to break our spirits.

The privatisation of the prison system in western states, in particular, the US is the new form of neo-colonial slavery, which allows profits and revenue generation as more blacks go into the prison system, the white man profits and is incentivised to imprison more black men like animals. Corporate investors in Wall Street, who generate revenue off prisoners' work, lobby for longer sentences, in order to expand their workforce, who can now compete with minimum wage companies in places such as China. Largely, US Anglo-Saxon corporations utilise these private prisons. For example, IBM, Boeing, Motorola, Microsoft, AT&T, Wireless, Texas Instrument, Dell, Compaq, Honeywell, Hewlett-Packard, Nortel, Lucent Technologies, 3Com, Intel, Northern Telecom, TWA, Nordstrom's, Revlon, Macy's, Pierre Cardin, and Target Stores[xxxviii].

An interesting example was when Pennsylvanian Judge Mark A. Ciavarella and Judge Michael Conahan, were paid more than $2.6 million from privately run youth centres owned by PA Child Care. [xxxix] A private prison contractor, who intentionally sent black children to prison, the aim was to keep these private profit generating prisons full with black people. Ciavarella, sent an African-American child to jail for three months for posting negative comments about her assistant principal on MySpace. Such brutality is a function of the dehumanisation of the black specimen by the Neo-Colonial Hollywood Mirrors. Black people who choose to do crime and sell drugs, argue that they refuse to work minimum wage jobs, as they are able to generate large sums of money from criminal proceeds. But this black mentality of quick money and short termism lacks foresight. When the black boy or black man is convicted of a crime, and is sentenced to jail for years, he will work menial jobs for hours on end for 30 cents an hour in prison, the question then becomes if this black man had decided to work a minimum wage job for 12 dollars an hour, instead of selling drugs and being convicted, in monetary terms he would have been far better off. This is simple financial planning and basic mathematics, but the black boy blinded by western materialism, the esteem of gang identity and the pursuit of the Neo-Colonial Hollywood Mirror falls into the white mans trap.

The Black Experience and Idealisations the White Man Has Created for the Black Child

The Neo-Colonial Hollywood Mirror allows for the glamorisation of this gangster/drug dealing lifestyle, which the white man has created for your black children to aspire to. It creates an identity for your child, a destructive self-determination, a gang, a family whereby he feels valued and accepted, and a place where he can exist as an equal, given that the hegemony of the white man has psychologically broken him.

It is important to note that, the environment that the white man has engineered for your black child's development is one, where he may rap about his toxic environment, given these are the tools that the white man places in the playground for a young black boy, given the power of the neo-colonial voice. This other black world creates entertainment for white children from less socially deprived areas and less violent backgrounds. When they listen to your black child rap about his pain, which in turn further conditions their perspectives on black people. That, which the white child finds so riveting, an alien black culture that entertains them, just as their white ancestors who were slave buyers, were entertained when inspecting naked black slaves for auction.

Let's take a brief and simplistic history lesson about the black experience: They have taken you from Africa and lied to the world arguing that our forefathers sold us to them, they have now taken your forefathers to a foreign land enslaved them on a cotton field, taken their identity and named and rebranded them like products, at a point when the Atlantic slave trade industry became less profitable they chose to give blacks their so-called freedom and invented segregation laws to keep you enslaved. Now there are a growing number of free black folk, as an option for the blacks the white man now creates the American Colonization Society, in order to send you back to Liberia, their dormant manufactured version of Africa. Now you are aware this isn't necessarily a viable option, you stay in the US the only place you have known your whole life. The white man now puts you in socially deprived areas, you cannot find a job as the white man won't employ you, given his acute racist psychology. The schools that you can afford to take your children to, won't equip or empower them to go to higher education.

However, you need to eat, the white man infests your demographically high black area with drugs, as he creates and involves himself with foreign wars of weaker nations, in the name of white righteous hegemony, the white man can't be seen to be supporting a rebel group, thus his agents sell cocaine, heroin to your black children for them to sell on the streets, so he can use the profits to fund the new slave kings he wishes to control as part of his neo-colonial empire. For example, the August 18–20, 1996 San Jose Mercury News published the Dark Alliance series by Gary Webb[xl] which held that: "For around a decade, the San Francisco Bay Area drug ring sold cocaine to the Crips and Bloods gangs of Los Angeles and siphoned millions of drug profits to a Latin American guerrilla army run by the U.S. CIA. This drug operation started the first pipeline between Colombia's cocaine cartels and the black neighbourhoods of Los Angeles, consequently, this influx of cocaine became the preeminent factor that started the crack epidemic in black communities."[xli]

Yet, the white man interestingly brands your black children whom he uses, as criminals and drugs dealers, and thereby the white man's righteous protector – the police – must shoot to kill your unarmed black children or imprison them. Have you not yet seen the cycle of entrapment and death that the white man has created for your black children?

Indeed, your black child may become famous and rap about the Neo-Colonial Hollywood Mirror – the idealisation of (money, cars, drugs), whilst doing two positive things for the white racial prejudice voice: 1) enriching the white man by selling records, now that he has signed you to his label that he owns, and: 2) you have fulfilled the self-perpetuating house nigger duties by glamorising violence, drugs, misogynism and importantly praising the vanity of material goods that the white man has created for you to aspire to, on the racial pyramid.

Rather than aspiring to be a part of black unity and rapping about building schools, universities, hospitals, rehabilitation centres, factories, making investments in property, companies and owning shares in Massa's record label yourself. Similar to ideas espoused by Jay-Z's record the story of OJ. Some may argue, but my label will tell me my

107

records won't sell, does it surprise you that Massa wants you to self-mutilate and assassinate your black character/identity and dignity, in order to perpetuate and reinforce messages about the Neo-Colonial Hollywood Mirror they have created to enslave your black people?

The black male trap is a common cycle, whereby your black child sells drugs and goes to the colonial prison, where he learns to be an animal, where he is raped, where he is beaten, where he cannot reproduce and have more black sons to pollute the beautiful white society – the black man genocide – now the white man looks down smiling at not only the spiral of black genocide he has created but at the ingenuity of it, itself.

Black men and women can you not see what the white man has done, can you not snap out of this magical yoke. This Neo-Colonial Hollywood Mirror has for so long blinded your ancestors, blinded your fathers and mothers that is now blinding your children.

Why is it that black boys, can kill another black boy, for looking at them walking down the street, because they are afraid of what the other black boy will see, their insecurity, their weakness, their fear, the black boy is prepared to kill and fight over this, as all his dignity has been taken from him, all that is left is his shame, his perception of being weak, becomes the only thing in this world that he feels he can control.

The black man or boy talks about his street gang, or his "homies" "dawgs" or in the UK "man dem", "boy dem" as his family, where he can earn a distorted form of respect and acceptance through the use of criminal currency. Yet, what they do not understand is that black males who ask their younger black brethren to join their street gang or sell drugs are again an extension of white neo-colonialism and black enslavement. For this is the self-inflicting identity destruction that the white man creates in his Neo-Colonial Hollywood Mirror, for the black boy to aspire to. This aspiration more often than not becomes a reality; the consequence is death or imprisonment. Remember, once the white man is able to derive and configure the parameters of your identity they can break and destroy you. Participating in black gang culture is the easiest way for the white man to control black males, it is a sub-culture that has been invented by the white man to destroy black men. Participation in this is to put the bullet in the pistol that has already been aimed at you since your birth.

Economic Colonial Chains, Rejoice in Black Self-Determination

In secondary school, it became clear to me that I was being broken as a black boy. In order for one to get into a good university in the UK, one needs to sit certain exam papers at the higher level, which would enable you to get the highest grades in order to get accepted into the right sixth forms/high schools/colleagues, which would propel you into the best universities. If you are not allowed to sit these higher papers, you will have to take the foundation or intermediary papers, which limited your ability to get the highest marks in the exam, in some instances the highest you could achieve was a "C", whereas for where I knew I was going I needed an "A*".

The point of the foundation (i.e. lower/intermediate) papers was to ensure that those less academically capable could still get satisfactory results. However, when you are a black child, and the psychological racial ideology by most white teachers, given the Neo-Colonial Hollywood Mirror is that you are less academically capable. And consequently, you are forced to take foundation papers, given the white man's hypnotisation of the belief in black inferiority. How does the black boy elevate his station? When he is repeatedly being intellectually repressed and is not given the opportunities to excel.

He has to possess a level of determination, and courage that needs to be nurtured and directed, otherwise, this can turn to anger, given that he is consistently being told no. This is very similar to the African-American student experience during the racial segregation era, where black schools emerged offering public elementary, junior and senior high schools. These schools offered several vocational courses such as cosmetology, tailoring and welding. Low skilled subjects that would not empower or allow black students to usefully elevate themselves.

I excelled at Science and continually got A*'s, and in this, my white science teacher was irritated and challenged me on multiple occasions, in front of the classroom asking me "whether I thought I was hard," to which I replied "no". In his subconscious, what he really meant by this question is, am I above you, do you accept my power over you, you black slave boy? He chose to intentionally lose my exam paper for a final exam, which inhibited my ability to pursue sciences at a higher level. You would think, why would a grown white man do that to a black child? The answer is to limit and destroy you before you become a black man. It is simply the hatred of the black race, which is driven from the reflection of the Neo-Colonial Hollywood Mirror.

Similarly, but at a later juncture of my life, when I worked in an Investment Bank. A senior member of staff, one of which was my mentor, said to me: "You should count yourself lucky to be working in this institution you know, coming from Ghana, you are lucky, I don't even care if your dad is the King of Ghana, you are lucky and I am giving you an opportunity".

I remember another senior banker mentioning to me that: "if my father was not the president, there was no point in him hiring me into his firm". On another occasion, whilst being bullied by my manager, and when flagging this, being told in my review that I was being defensive. It became clear to me that these men in positions of power did not recognise my experience and talent as a prerequisite to me getting my job. Rather, they were more focused on what the colour of my black skin meant, in their minds. Although I had more qualifications and experience than my peer group, like a good black slave, I should have been thankful to Massa in their minds for the opportunity they bestowed me with.

The white man largely employs black people to fill quotas – positive discrimination, they employ you, and torture you like an animal in a cage until you leave, or they tell you that you have underperformed. Subconsciously in their white superior psyche you are: (effectively a lazy field nigger who hasn't met his cotton-picking quota, and therefore deserves to be whipped), that you are being defensive: (effectively an angry black man who needs to be tamed like a wild bull), you are incapable of performing your job: (effectively you are not as intelligent as your white counterparts, because you are black and more akin to the intelligence of an animal).

Understand my brothers, the more wisdom or intelligence that you have as a black man, the more painful your experience will be, white men hate intelligent black men, or rather black men they cannot manipulate. You are better off being a gangster or an unintelligent black man with a lower IQ which fits into the model of their mental depictions of black men. That which the Neo-Colonial Hollywood Mirror, has taught them to believe. When you as a black man come up with an innovative idea, or ask an intelligent question or can think out of the box, whether that be in a board room or classroom, they do not want to hear your voice, in fact, they pretend not to hear you, in some cases they are so astounded that you came up with a brilliant idea, they create excuses in their minds to account for the occurrence, "oh it must have been by accident." The white mind has been so hypnotised by the idealisation that they are superior and are the best, that their minds won't allow them to hear the voice of an individual they subconsciously view as a black animal, in fact, in some cases they struggle to make eye contact because they are that uncomfortable.

The Neo-Colonial Hollywood Mirror disassociates black skin with quality or professionalism, if there are more black people in a workplace or area, psychologically the global community disavows this phenomenon as lower quality. Even in business meetings, black people themselves only take another black businessman seriously if they see white colleagues, with white skin, so powerful is this Neo-Colonial Hollywood Mirror. For example, in the third quarter of 2018, African-American workers had the highest unemployment rate nationally, at (6.3 percent), followed by Hispanics (4.5 percent) and whites (3.2 percent).[xlii]

The highest African-American unemployment rate is in the District of Columbia (12.4 percent), followed by Illinois (9.3 percent), Louisiana (8.5 percent), Alabama (7.1 percent), and New York (7.0 percent). Whilst, the highest Hispanic state unemployment rate is in Nebraska (5.9 percent), followed by Connecticut (5.7 percent), Arizona (5.6 percent), Pennsylvania (5.6 percent), and Washington (5.6 percent).

Meanwhile, the highest white state unemployment rate is (5.0 percent,) in West Virginia.[xliii]

Even in the criminal world the leaders of, "successful" black criminal organisations are referred to as kingpins, rather than the mafia, mob, crime families, a cartel, or organised crime units, titles and esteems preferred for non-black criminals. The psychologically inbred perception is that non-black criminals are smarter criminals, than their black counterparts, and therefore are identified with greater esteem than just "gangster", (i.e. they are interpolated as higher in status on the criminal racial pyramid).

Consequently, the white man justifies their unfair treatment of blacks by paying you less, giving you no bonus, firing you, a simple reinforcement of the Neo-Colonial Hollywood Mirror. In their white neo-colonial racist mentalities, you deserve this treatment because you are black, you shouldn't be here, and you are lucky to be here, your suffering is just an excuse, you need to be punished, you black slave is what dwells persistently in their subconscious white superior psyche syndrome minds, like an irritable rash, which is reinforced by the Neo-Colonial Hollywood Mirror.

White superiority after colonialism, with the imposition of puppet African leaders who were forced to model their laws on British, French, Spanish or Portuguese laws, eradicated African political identity and enforced white forms of government which was used to enslave our future black leaders, children and stifled economic development. The simple illusion of democracy, and subsequently the so-called African emancipation (decolonisation) or the more recent Arab spring. Effectively, the white man using the Neo-Colonial Hollywood Mirror to re-create the perfect obedient assimilating African or Arab, to steal their natural resources, in order for them to submit to foreign invaders whilst overthrowing their own brothers, permitted and aided in current times because of the greed of a few Arab and black leaders.

One fact that I feel is important to note about the Neo-Colonial Hollywood Mirror, is that if it fails to blind consciousness and fails to create assimilating identities. There are economic and political levers, intertwined with military/police power that act as hard enforcers of the white mans will. For example, the dollar is the most widely used currency in the human global community. The US Department of Justice has put in place legal parameters to extradite crimes involving the US dollar for prosecution on US soil. Using its economic currency as a means to supersede national state sovereignty and international rule of law. Parallels can be drawn to the International Criminal Court (ICC), arguably created to imprison and control former Black African leaders, note that not one Western leader has ever been held accountable for their crimes against humanity in this court. Importantly, major powers, including the United States, UK, France, Russia and China, are beyond the court's reach because they have veto power over the council's decisions.

Similarly, economic sanctions applied by the US, EU to other nation-states, is done to force them to submit to the Neo-Colonial Hollywood economic mirror. For example, we have seen this with North Korea, Russia, Iran and China. What we can see is that the Western States have no intention of relinquishing economic power after colonialism, rather it is economic control that allows them to create identities for their inferior Black African economic powers. For example, since 1945, the West African and Central African states have pegged their currencies (CFA) to the French francs and thereafter the Euro, with their financial reserves kept in France.

The Central African bloc of countries that use the CFA includes: Chad, Central African Republic, Congo Republic, Gabon, Cameroon and Equatorial Guinea. This policy has kept African economies largely dependent on the European monetary policy, a form of economic neo-colonialism. With the subconscious ideological undertones being that black African leaders cannot manage state money or the economy. Between African states they would rather transact in foreign American or European currencies than use their own, this consequently means it is difficult for African countries to trade amongst each other and easy for Western states to manipulate their currencies, particularly in trade. Pre-colonial Africa, had a common form of currency, by which tribes could trade freely amongst one another. For example, Manillas was a currency primarily used in West Africa, usually made from bronze or copper. During colonial rule in Nigeria, the Native Currency Proclamation in 1902 outlawed the import of Manillas unless the British High Commissioner permitted it. This was done to encourage the use of coined British West African currency, brought in to displace Manillas currency.

Importantly, British West African currency could be floated against British and French currency, allowing Western trading companies to manipulate their value to their advantage, based on supply and demand[xliv]. This couldn't be done as easily with Manillas, an economic system needed to be put in place, to be able to control the colonised concept of value. Therefore, in 1948, the British administration replaced Manillas with British West African currency. The Manillas stopped being a form of currency in British West Africa on April 1st, 1949[xlv]. It is interesting in current times, how nothing has evolved from this Native Currency proclamation, black African states are still economically in chains, and the inbred subconscious psychology of black African statesmen is that they cannot function, without the white man. This is driven by the subservient historical conditioning and development over time of the colonial mirror.

This parallels the Tulsa Massacre in Oklahoma, what was referred to as "black wall street", an area which alluded to "wall street" where current-day financial institutions house their businesses in New York. Note that, in modern American society there is no modern-day "black wall street". Note also, how in the streets of Accra, in Ghana, roads are called "oxford street", this plays on the perception of economic power and success, and the attempt of the black mind to innately mimic white economic success, rather than creating their own.

Importantly, during this period, black Americans became economically independent by largely investing within their communities and spending on their own black-owned businesses. Greenwood residents selected their own leaders and raised capital there to support economic growth. Given that Jim Crow laws did not allow black Americans to buy or use services in white areas, this had the reverse effect of creating economic independence for black Americans in that region.

White Americans in that city grew increasingly resentful about the wealth of the Greenwood community. The Tulsa

Race Massacre of 1921 was sparked when the police accused a Black shoe-shiner of "assaulting" a white woman, resulting in the black shoe shiner being lynched. The result was white Americans attacking black neighbourhoods and killing, burning and looting stores and homes. About 10,000 black people were left homeless, and property damage amounted to more than $1.5 million in real estate and $750,000 in personal property (equivalent to the cost of $32.25 million in 2019)[xlvi]. Private planes were also used to shoot black Americans, as well as to burn buildings. Here, we must note that the racial pyramid and the Neo-Colonial Hollywood Mirror only works if the black race is in pursuit of white economic, social "success" and materials. If the black race is successful in their own right and asserts their own self-determination, the backstop which is the military lever (i.e. police, National Guard), will be employed to restore this order, this order being black economic and political inferiority.

Identity Creation of Nation States

The white man has imposed racial superiority not just on a micro, but macro level. Using the Neo-Colonial Hollywood Mirror to racialise hierarchically states. Look at Saudi Arabia, Israel, and South Korea these states have killed and massacred in the name of the White man and so have many other states, as they have bought into the illusion of the racial pyramid and the US righteous hegemony. When western Anglo-Saxon states only intervene in the affairs of foreign nations for the economic interests of their states, we saw this recently with Trump deploying US troops to protect oil assets in Syria. It is interesting because foreign wars are mostly covertly engineered by the white man, the objective to keep other states economically and socially destroyed. Just such that they are always in the pursuit of the white man's support as inferior entities, unable to manage and control their populations.

The Neo-Colonial Hollywood Mirror applies to the identity creation of nation-states. For example, does it even make any logical sense to have a UN security council with five permanent members in a global community of 197 nation-states, does it make sense for sanctions to be applied by the stronger military/economic nations to the weak? How do we hold strong states like P-5 members and the US accountable? Have you ever heard of a situation whereby sanctions were enforced on the United States, Britain, and France for crimes against humanity by other states for accidental drone attacks on civilians, schools and hospitals? If a notion such as this is unfathomable to you, understand the power that the cloak of the Neo-Colonial Hollywood Mirror has, in shaping your thoughts about the world and your ideas of yourself.

Indeed, it is very similar to the language identity tools, sanctioned by Uncle Sam used to justify acts of war, using the Neo-Colonial Hollywood Mirrors via the media to socialise the ideology of other nation-states as "the axis of evil", "war on terror", "rogue nations", "mad man with a rocket" these sentences are fabrications based on lies of the neo-colonial power, capitulating themselves as the righteous hegemon, the superior, and by extension, they have the right to fight their holy war, and righteously kill the other who they have created through their juggernaut IT hegemonic global media refractions.

You see, once the white man is able to depict you as the other, abnormal, and unusual, something opposed to the norms and rules they set, they can use their media and colonial voices to recreate identities and re-write history. In fact, they can transform anything and anyone into a sub-class human being, a sub-class state, once the white man does this and you are the other, he can kill you with impunity, even the so-called liberals will applaud him.

Fundamentally, we are subconscious slaves to the Neo-Colonial Hollywood Mirror, and this is how the white man has been able to conquer the world twice over and break states, because we reveal our fallibility and it is simply our attempts of assimilation to the white man's dream, falling in love with the Neo-Colonial Hollywood Mirror and the racial pyramid and the pursuit of assimilatory white human perfection. I ask you, my humble brothers, to let us rediscover our black consciousness, and let us develop our own mirrors that reflect our likeness.

For example, think about atoms packed into a tight container, now heat the container and look at the assimilation and movement we see of the atoms, imagine the stronger atoms survive and we repeat this experiment, and again the stronger atoms survive. Now imagine we inject new atoms, who have had the hindsight of seeing weaker atoms disappear, they will assimilate to the stronger atoms once put in the same container, in order to survive under the same conditions.

Now look at the current world now, look what happened, to Iraq, Iran, Afghanistan, Syria, Yemen, Libya, and Somalia when these weaker atoms didn't assimilate to the whims of the stronger atoms, the United States, United Kingdom, France, Germany, Israel, Japan and Saudi Arabia. Note in this example, heat is the external facilitator, needed to be applied to create assimilation with the atoms, it is clear that the white man has used as an external facilitator his economic might, police brutality, military and media prowess to enforce assimilation to the Neo-colonial Hollywood Mirror by force and death if necessary. This structure is strengthened with the idealisation of the white man as Massa, which plays on the subconscious mind. It is almost similar to being in a state of prolonged hypnosis, by the psychological Neo-Colonial Hollywood Mirror holder – the white man.

Whether it be at the Governmental level with African leaders unwisely spending more on space programs and military weapons at the white man's behest, or allowing the establishment of US neo-colonial military bases on their soil. This is because African leaders have psychologically fallen in love with the Neo-Colonial Hollywood Mirror, and are bound by the yoke of self-grandeur, idealisations and rules by which the white man has set. In an environment where people in African nations can't afford to eat or die because they do not have sufficient medical facilities. In this way, the white man has replaced the physical chains on our dark ivory necks and ankles, with shackles that stem from the re-creation of our black identities, through which the Neo-Colonial Hollywood Mirror keeps us psychologically enslaved through the media, which gags and destroys our unpolluted black dreams and identities.

Are you aware of how they tortured President Obama? How dare the white man ask their elected leader of a nation-state to show proof of his birth? They felt justified in his belittlement and humiliating exercise of power because president Obama is a black man. Would they have compelled a white leader by force to show such proof of his identity? Have they even asked Donald Trump to show proof of his identity, his taxes? Have they even cleared his name or asked for proof that he didn't sexually assault the multiple women that have come forward against him? Let me again ask you a question, if such cases had been positioned against President Obama would he have been shown such grace? That steep racial pyramid that is embedded within the Neo-Colonial Hollywood Mirror is so bright and blinding that most citizens can't see through the injustice and white privilege.

The ability of the white man to create black identities enabled the destruction of Kwame Nkrumah, Ghana's first president. Remember, through the power of the Neo-Colonial Hollywood Mirror, the white man imprisoned Mandela, and in the next breath when it suited the West, they made him an international beacon of light. Similarly, they destroyed the identity of Libya's Gaddafi for advocating for a United Africa, one individual who took a stand against the US military-industrial complex. We must control our African narrative and ensure that we do not allow the white man's vanity, materials, so-called righteous hegemony and IT hegemony blind our minds, identity and subconscious psyche.

We must break free from the poisonous colonial chains and strive for equality amongst all men, whether we are in the US, Russia, UK, France, Germany, China or India. Let this hypnotic imprisonment of delusions of who we are as black men and women diminish. Let the sanctity of our black consciousness and determination break free, from the hypnotic Neo-Colonial Hollywood Mirrors that entrance and mesmerise the black race. Like a lost cat chasing its tail, round and round in loose circles, trapped by the illusion of the reflection of itself in the Neo-Colonial Hollywood Mirror. Our black minds are a key component of our consciousness, and it has been attacked and broken. Yet, our black spirits are unbreakable, through black unity we can re-shape our dilapidated identities the white man has destructively created for us. Our consciousness is key to our sanity, what becomes consistently reinforced (i.e. The Neo-Colonial Hollywood Mirror) begins to shape our minds and numb our black consciousness, robbing our sanity.

Similar to a rape victim, we begin to blame ourselves, seeking alternatives to the brute reality of our humiliation and failure as black men to protect ourselves from violation. We must first begin to love ourselves in our core black essence and speak our truths, this process is called black re-identification. Fear not, the salty tears that you cry, the acidic burden of your pain, your feeling of nothingness. Every tear that dribbles loosely down your black face, are the silky cords that you need to re-connect you to the umbilical cord, our black nutrients that house our pure black identity. Free of pain, free of rape, free of escapism through drugs, alcohol and violence. Importantly, my black brothers, we must forgive the white man for the destruction he engineered, for if we continue to hate and blame the white man, he drains our blessings, our happiness, we feed his neo-colonial soul and power. The black man genocide is a current-day pathology that we must destroy, through a renewed black re-identification within ourselves and communities.

In this deconstruction of humanities domineering voice, I must say: Black men, we are not entertainers, we are not athletes, we are leaders, we are business owners, we are lovers, where is our black self-determination? We need to redefine our black history, our black philosophy, and our black spirits, in the reconstruction of black unity. In order for Africa to be healed, we must unite and trade within ourselves. We must not sit there ideally watching the US flex its economic muscles in order to stop the economic rise of China, think about your black children, their children and create a union such that we do not have to bow to the whip of Massa the white man or whether this is the Chinese Massa in the future.

We must be conscious of the fact that, in order for the black man to have attained the degree of freedoms enjoyed in Western states, there have been centuries of black liberation movements, conflicts, deaths at the hands of our white oppressors. This black civil rights struggle has not yet occurred with the East who are growing in power. As they grow in power, they will displace the US as an IT hegemon, and possess the ability to shape identities. Remember, currently given the Neo-Colonial Hollywood Mirror we as black people are perceived at the bottom of the racial pyramid. When the superpower baton is reluctantly passed to China, this will not change the positions of black people with the ascent of Asiatic superpowers.

Particularly with the majority of African states receiving financing in exchange for their natural resources from China. We need to be asking ourselves, how will African nations and the black race lift itself up from foreign control and the imposition of inferiority? Note that the power of the Neo-Colonial Hollywood Mirror is so powerful, even with the dissent of the West, the West has structured this mirror such that the black race is eternally damned, at the bottom of the racial pyramid, even amongst other races of colour. Unless we as black people rise up to break this distorted mirror, we will always be treated as subservient inferior species, even with the ascension of new Asian powers.

Black Cultural Language Edification

Education has been developed and shaped by the perception of the white man's colonial mirror of the world, education is a weapon that can be used to shape the mind. History has been told from a Eurocentric[xlvii] perspective, the black man's definition of success is pinned against the aspirations of the white man's designs. We must teach our black brethren that to be successful, is not to acquire the white man's wealth and goods or to assimilate to their world and become what you view as elite. But rather we must teach each other to reinvest in our black communities and to help each other, rise up. Post-colonialism saw the physical dissent of colonial powers from Africa, yet their hold on the Africans mind has remained intact. This was primarily achieved through education, which colours perception, our psyches and therefore our truths and realities.

For example, in European colonies, religious missions were instrumental in introducing European narratives of education, particularly in shaping the ideology of inferiority to the black mind. Roman Catholic Missionaries, the Society for the Propagation of the Gospel, the Moravian Mission, the Mission of Breme and the Methodists, established missionaries in the Gold Coast (current-day Ghana) between the years 1820–1881. Similarly, in Nigeria, Protestant missionaries were opened at Badagry, Abeokuta, Lagos, and Bonny between the years 1860–1899. In Uganda and Kenya, the Church Missionary Society, the Universities Mission to Central Africa, and the London Missionary Society opened the first mission schools in 1840 and 1900.

The majority of educational establishments were run by colonial powers, this allowed the psyche of the African child to be shaped, allowing for the creation of mental assimilation and subservience to the white colonial master[xlviii]. The educational system inherited from colonial rule, inbred a racial inferiority complex, which created assimilation to the perceived superior white colonial rulers. In primary education, the English, Spanish or French language, preceded African languages, which became the official language of African states despite the use of local dialect by the masses. This created a hierarchy within black identities, what was conceived as the black African elite was effectively demarcated by certain facets, one being the ability to speak English or French in likeness or as close to the white man as possible.

Psychologically this elevated the black man's social standing within the black social pyramid, by black social pyramid, I mean a formation of black class, white attributes that the black man attains (European language, university degrees, elite government seats, suits), in likeness or in the pursuit of his white counterpart.

All of this, ties back to the central point that the black race needs to take hold of education and formulate its own criterions of class, education, success, society and community. For black people, the philosophy of ancient

Greece (Socrates and Plato), needs to be replaced by the philosophy of Africans (Egypt's Ptahhotep and Tanzania's, Ujamaa, Ethiopia's Zera Yacob, and Senegambia's, Maxuréja Demba Xolé Faal), to name a few. Who debunk by virtue of being African, the notion that the black man, cannot think for himself. What we realise is that the white man's perception of the black species as untamed, aggressive, lazy doesn't hold weight. One only has to look to the ancient African philosophical paradigms that formed the basis of the past. For example, concepts such as Omoluwabi[xlix], which represents courage, humility and respect, where ideologies that informed communal behaviour and interactions of ancient black identities, namely modern-day peoples of Akan – (Ghana, Ivory Coast), Dogon (Mali, Burkina Faso), Serer (Senegal. Gambia and Mauritania) and Dahomey (Benin).

The view of the French colonial power was: *Colonial duty and political necessity impose a double task on our education work: on the one hand, it is a matter of training an indigenous staff destined to become our assistants throughout the domains and to assure the ascension of a carefully chosen elite, and on the other hand, it is a matter of educating the masses, to bring them nearer to us and to change their way of life.* (From Bulletin de l'Enseignment en AOF, No. 74, 1931)[l]. It is this psychological perception that still has not changed in modern times. Given the protest in relation to the George Floyd killing, and actions such as taking down statues with racial histories and connotations. Allowing black people into elite positions in corporations or governments, will not change the mind of humanities racialised lenses, which has been informed by the Neo-Colonial Hollywood Mirror. Instead, it is the psychological conditioning of the mind, the recreation of humanities mind, to disassociate inferiority with the black race that must be achieved and tackled.

Have you wondered, why we as African descendants, refer to ourselves as "black," in fact throughout this whole deconstruction I have referred to us as "Black man" and "Black woman". The term "black" which translates into Spanish as "negro", did not have negative connotations when this word came into use. Rather it had Indo-European origins, the term, "black" (meant fire, shining white, or flashing in various bright colours), which was void of negative association and without racial connotations.

The negative connotation and invention of the term "black people" by European imperialists, stemmed from the need for Africans to be dehumanised in order to enslave them. The term "nigger", "negro", "coloured", "black", and now "people of colour", "BAME", are used to create a subconscious form of alienation, which allows wicked acts to be perpetuated. Given that referring to Africans by their ancestral tribal identities (Ashanti, Fanti, Ewe, Yoruba, Benga, Igbo, and Mandinka etc) forces one to recognise our humanity, rich history and culture.

The idea behind labelling a human being is to forge their identities, what the Europeans and Americans have done to our people is to create a label, they can control, add attributes and use as a way to control us. This eradication of our ancestral identities, and the acceptance of our new identities by the white man, means that we have subconsciously agreed to let them control our destinies. In fact, we should not even be referring to Caucasian people as white; it gives them more power, as this term white is again, an identity they have forged and one, which has given them privileges. As they have used language as a means to shape the psychological perception of the majority of races in this world.

The biggest mistake that we as descendants of Africa can make is accepting this label, which negatively creates our identities.

For me, "black" and "negro" are synonymous with each other. They are inherently derogatory labels – imposed on Africans to diminish their humanity and to repress our people[li].

For our forefathers in Africa never created or had a term such as "black", "negro" or "person of colour" prescribed to them, so why should we as free men accept this? We are our ancestral identities. We must learn to create our own labels, our own identities, and tell the Americans and Europeans what we will be referred to as.

A school and university for black people must be developed to re-educate and re-edify black minds, where black children can learn about their histories, cultures, their identities, and how history and identity creation, has created the society in which they live in now.

Free from the political, economic and philosophical constraints of the white man's voice. Saturday classes must be reinstated for black children, where identity can be re-taught to them, void of manipulation, contempt and harassment of the white educational institution. Indeed, a university must be built and dedicated to our black children, to our forefathers and heritage. This university must be called, Sankofa which translates to "Go back and get it". In the Ghanaian Twi Language, meaning we as a black race need to understand our histories, re-educate ourselves, and recreate our identities. As a black race, we need to understand that our heritage and identities are what the white man created and named Africa, what was originally termed Alkebu-lan by our forefathers. As African diaspora, our vacations and holidays should not be spent, on pursuing and exploring the cities of powerful Western nations, who had their wealth, marble statues, roads, and bridges created of the back of black slaves. But rather, we must return to Africa to explore our identities and roots, in order to truly understand who, we are.

My brothers and sisters, we must edify our language and eliminate the colonial undertones. Remember, identity is created through language, language informs and colours the mind, and our mind colours our perception and consequently our experience of reality. Language that was formerly used to characterise our identity by colonial force, for example, the word "nigger", used by slave owners and the removal of our birth right, by the eradication of our natural African names were tools used to eradicate black self-determination and our original black African identities.

Interestingly, now black Americans use this same language as a cornerstone of their perceived black culture, which the white man has engineered and created for them. And when the black American is questioned, it is argued: we call it taking back power, feeling empowered to use such words such as calling ourselves niggers, which were used to confine our identities.

Yet, by continuing the usage of such language identity parameters that the white man has used to psychologically create and repress black identities, we are continually reinforcing racial inferiority, by tying ourselves to an inferior identity complex that the white man created for us. For example, when a rebellious slave would run away, he would be re-captured, and the terminology bitch nigger would be used to characterise him, because the slaver owners would rape the slave in front of the entire black slave community, to humiliate, disgrace and rebrand in a reductionist manner that slave's self-worth, creating a broken identity – one of shame, used as a tool of mutilation in order evaporate the idea of rebellion. Similar to ethnic cleaning and the use of sexual violence as a means to perpetuate fear and eradicate rebellion.

Relatedly, the use of the term "motherfucker" a language identity parameter created by the white slave owners to eradicate the self-identity and self-worth of the black man, which further eradicated black traditional family models. This was another form of denigration through the use of language creating identity parameters. Slave owners would breed slaves like cattle – effectively, sexual reproduction centres. For example, a slave would be forced to have sex with his mother, his sister, his cousin, her uncle, her brother, her father and her son. In order to reproduce black slave children, the motivation was to generate profit for white slave owners. For example, Virginia law in 1662 ruled that the station of the child would follow the status of the enslaved mother, which meant that enslaved women gave birth to generations upon generations of black slave children now seen as slave commodities.

These persistent indictments become socialised and internalised psychologically over centuries of enforcement by Massa, the self-worth of the black male and females becomes reduced to a sex slave and this pathology continues in the black men's so-called freedom. These facets become paralleled and linked by images refracted by the Neo-Colonial Hollywood Mirror and pornographic imagery of the black man, linked to bestiality, untamed sex, large genitalia, animals, and these images all refract abnormal or extra-terrestrial white propaganda on the black boy's psyche causing confusion, which eradicates human characteristics and hence makes the black man void of human identification, and subsequent violence and abuse become justified and normalised.

Please note that in this historical context, the destruction of the black traditional family structure. As a black slave and a "motherfucker" you were never with your family in a traditional family male role setting, you were never with one woman as you were forced to reproduce with multiple slave women, even your own family members. This pathology and ideology in current times is reflected in the depiction of "black men as cheaters".

Similarly, black slave men having multiple children with different slave women by force becomes reflected in the ideology in current times of the black man with multiple "baby mamas". Note also that in current times, the mass incarceration of black men means when they come out of prison their families are broken or their partners move on, such that he will consistently find new partners, particularly if he goes to prison multiple times. This mirrors, black slaves not being at home in the traditional family setting, as there was no existence of a traditional home or family structure on a slave plantation, just assimilatory attempts of emulating Massa and his family structure. Note, when I speak of traditional family structure, I mean – mother and father co-habituating in a marital structure with children produced from the same biological bloodline.

Central to all of this is overarching circular patterns of pathology, parallels can be drawn to a mother who has her child at 15, then in turn that child grows up to also have a child at 15. In the same way, the mother who is sexually molested by a family member as a child, her daughter or son grows up to have been also sexually molested by a family member. Similarly, the black slave boy who had no role model or father in his life, as his black slave father was on the field picking cotton, or in the house serving Massa, or indeed a sex slave in a camp effectively the "motherfucker".

In the same way, his son grows up to have children and is an absent role model for his son in current black society. The majority of black men do not know how to be fathers, because their pathologies much like their own have been perpetually broken and shattered, we as black men must teach ourselves and re-edify our minds on how to be fathers. Make no mistake, this chain of pathology is generational and stems from colonial subjugations that led to the destruction of the traditional black family structure and our lack of identity. We need to break these pathologies and circles of chains in our families, by re-edifying our language, which will re-edify our psyches and current ontological identities as a black race. Remember the habits you create define you.

Importantly, language creates identity, and the perpetual repetition of negative Neo-Colonial Hollywood language identity creation permeates our minds, self-worth and realities. We as a black race must edify our language. Black cultural norms, which subconsciously shapes modern black identities, for example, cultural norms such as referring to our people as 'niggers' and 'negroes,' 'motherfuckers' keeps us psychologically repressed and our identities mired underneath the racial pyramids which breaks our spirits and unity. It is interesting that the black man currently takes such repressive and dangerous lexicon 'niggers' and 'negroes,' 'motherfuckers' and makes it the cornerstone of their everyday interactions with each other culturally and then berates the white man in current times for using the language they created to confine our identities for the sake of their imperialism, for the sake of profit and for the sake of wickedness.

Now, we as physically free black men and women use such language as a part of our societal culture, what idiocy! What right do we have to tell white people not to use the "n" word because they are white and created it in our oppression, if we now as physically free black men use it to oppress ourselves? Simply put, it is reductionist in nature and nonsensical, the equivalent of saying 1-1=3. I ask you, black brothers and sisters, during the holocaust that characterised a horrific component of the Jewish experience, do you hear the Jews in current times using language that the Nazi's employed to repress and take away their identity? Do they address each other by quoting their parents, great grandparents holocaust numbers that were tattooed on their arms? We as a black race need to embrace our new identity, by breaking pathologies and language enforcing parameters, which subconsciously ties us to colonial chains.

Black men and women, we should be referring to our people as "champions", our women as "queens" and daughters as "achievers" our sons as "warriors". Language is the cornerstone of the fabric of the black community, it is through language that we will rediscover our identities, it is through language that we will be able to break the pathology that has allowed the white man to tie our minds in mental enslavement. It is through language that we will truly know ourselves unaltered from the poisonous paintbrush of the Neo-Colonial Hollywood Mirror.

We must allocate and make time for weekly sessions in our curriculums, where we discuss, evaluate and create, the image of what a black person is, and invert the white man's Neo-Colonial Hollywood Mirror. We must re-conceptualise and reengineer the image of the black man and woman, which has been projected onto the global community for centuries. In reconstructing our identities, it is only the seduction of western capitalism and greed that can destroy the re-engineering of our black race. So black people, we must learn to sacrifice, we must learn to stick together, we must learn who we are outside of this seductive colonial mirror.

But We Are Still Standing

Black fathers, yes, I know the majority of you had no example of fatherhood, I know the majority of you only knew the love of your mother or grandmother, I know you have been broken and blinded, mentally, psychologically and physically. But try for your generations to come, to guide your black boys, and teach them about their identity, about themself, about the Neo-Colonial Hollywood paintbrush that awaits them in the heat of the desert. Educate them to be ambitious, but to have goals in order to achieve them.

Yes, brothers, I know you are lost, your spirit is faint, ask the holy father to escape this material world, ask him to help you escape this emptiness, the allure of the immoral woman or man, the allure of Hollywood's Neo-Colonial Mirror, the allure of drugs and alcohol, the allure of the subconsciously embedded demarcations of the white man. Our black eyes are open, but psychologically our eyelids have been closed for centuries, coloured by the identity, ideas, hopes and assimilatory dreams the white man created for us, in order to control black men. In the same way, our ancestors' eyes were opened when the white man used the wood from our shores in Africa to build the ships to imprison, and ship us to their land and enslave us.

If I told you a delicate secret from the salty brown lips of a 10-year-old black boy, would you believe me? That being, the white race has woven discord, confusion, division and lies into the mouths, eyes, hearts and spirits of its forged nation-state followers through his re-drawing of state lines and the re-creation of ethnic tribes by force. He has molested morality, righteousness and taken our identity and pride, politically, socially and economically with the policies he creates. If for just one moment this could be the truth, would you allow Uncle Sam to still hold your bright mantle, your beacon for hope, his fabricated democracy and freedom? Would you still aspire to be Uncle Sam's foot soldier on the perceived wars of terror, he intentionally creates in order to feed his military-industrial complex and lagging economy?

God of Solomon, I am with you, God I am a black man, I seek not recognition but peace from those who have stolen my innocence, blinded my vision, sent ivory steel planes in the sky to rob my future, heavenly father, intervene for my sanity. How my stomach pounds, guzzles, twists and turns. How my poverty blinds and deceives me, how my father deserted and left me, how my father robbed what my family could have been. I pray that my father forgives the evil of his father and my, father's father, and his father before him.

I sit here and think of the Ashanti tale of the first form of Ghanaian female emancipation, the heroism of the Ashanti Queen Ya santewa, who chose to continue to fight the British invaders in spite of the technological advantage the Western forces had, she demanded: "If you, the men of Ashanti will not go forward, then we will. We, the women will. I shall call upon you my fellow women. We will fight the white men. We will fight until the last of us falls on the battlefield."[lii] It was this display of intrepidness shown by the Ashanti females that spurred the Black males to fight. Remember it is black female strength, which evokes the greatest strength of the black man. Whatever interpretation that one undertakes, it does not distract from the fact that whatever strength that black women bring to any situation; it has the power to transform black men.

This is my parting poem, brothers and sisters: the black man is angry, but yet void of rage, the black man is sad but full of hope with no clear paths to achieve his rage and the black woman is proud but full of rage, angry but full of hope, tired but full of pain. Without self-determination, the black man and black woman, are mutually exclusive, and simply fail to co-exist. If a spiritual rope tied a Black Queen to her Black King, a lack of identity would erode the spiritual rope, can't you see, love is in the eye of the beholder, if we fail to understand our identities and black self-determination, how can love be in the eye of our beholden?

Endnotes

[i] Preeminent race, a race who exudes an overwhelming amount of political, economic and social might. Whose ideologies are followed by other races around the world, given historical foreign policies, slavery, colonialism and international war campaigns, to preserve their pre-eminence

[ii] racism is defined "As any attitude, action, or institutional structure which subordinates a person or group because of his or their colour" (Racism in America, n.d., p.5)

[iii] Bausch, K. (2013). Superflies into Superkillers: Black Masculinity in Film from Blaxploitation to New Black Realism. Journal of Popular Culture, 46(2), 257–276.

[iv] Luther, C., Ringer Lepre, C., & Clark, N. (2012). Diversity in U.S. Mass Media. Malden: Wiley-Blackwell.

[v] Barlow, K. (2011, November 10). Hlismow media portray African-American males. University of Pittsburgh University Times.Retrieved October 6, 2014, from
http://www.utimes.pitt.edu?p=18764

[vi] Desert Sun, Volume 42, Number 296, 16 July 1969

[vii]https://libcom.org/files/Race%20Traitor%2001%20(1993%20Win ter).pdf (Writing in Issue 3 of Race Traitor in 1993)

[viii] Ariela Schachter, From "Different" to "Similar": An Experimental Approach to Understanding Assimilation, Published September 2, 2016

[ix] Bruce D. Jones, Peacemaking, S. 17 f; Carsten Heeger, Die Erfindung, S. 23–25

[x] Ranger T. (1993) The Invention of Tradition Revisited: The Case of Colonial Africa. In: Ranger T., Vaughan O. (eds) Legitimacy and the State in Twentieth-Century Africa. St Antony's/Macmillan Series. Palgrave Macmillan, London

[xi] https://www.aljazeera.com/indepth/opinion/berlin-1884-remembering-conference-divided-africa-191115110808625.html

[xii] Gourevitch, Philip (2000), We Wish To Inform You That Tomorrow We Will Be Killed With Our Families (Reprint ed.). London; New York: Picador

[xiii] Media is defined as: Communication channels through which news, entertainment, education, data, or promotional messages are disseminated. Media includes every broadcasting and narrowcasting medium such as newspapers, magazines, TV, radio, billboards, direct mail, telephone, fax, and internet. (Media, 2014, paragraph 1), "Media." Business Dictionary. 2014.

[xiv] Defined as, the people or nations of the world, considered as being closely connected by modern telecommunications and as being economically, socially, and politically interdependent

[xv] Information Technology Hegemon, is a nation-state who possesses significant media, social media corporations, networks, artificial intelligence, technology, that gives them the preponderant power to influence human ideas, perspectives and the ability to create identities

[xvi] https://www.metrotimes.com/newshits/archives/2019/07/1 2/detro it-cops-arrest-police-commissioner-protester-at-raucous-public- meeting

[xvii] Refers to Leadership; preponderant influence or authority; usually applied to the relation of a government or state to its neighbors or confederates. (cf. Webster's Revised Unabridged Dictionary, G. & C. Merriam, 1913)

[xviii] Carmichael, John (1993). African Eldorado – Gold Coast to Ghana. Gerald Duckworth & Co. Ltd. pp. 176–77

[xix] https://www.sousterandhicks.com/where-suits-originated.html

[xx] https://www.businessinsider.com/why-gucci-clothes-racist- blackface-sambo-2019-2?r=US&IR=T

[xxi] https://www.nytimes.com/2019/02/07/business/gucci-blackface- adidas-apologize.html

[xxii] https://www.bbc.co.uk/news/magazine-35240987

[xxiii] https://www.independent.co.uk/news/world/africa/sold-as-a- slave-exhibited-as-a-freak-sarah-finds-dignity-after-200-years- 172810.html

[xxiv] U.S. Bureau of Justice Statistics, Prisoners in 2016, 8 tbl.6 (Jan. 2018)

[xxv] Marc Mauer, Addressing Racial Disparities in Incarceration, 91 supp. 3 The Prison Journal 87S, 88S (Sept. 2011)

[xxvi] FBI Uniform Crime Reporting Program. Crime in the United States 2016

[xxvii] Puzzanchera, C., Sladky, A. and Kang, W. (2017). Easy Access to Juvenile Populations: 1990–2016; OJJDP Statistical Briefing Book

[xxviii] Ghandnoosh, N. (2014). Race and Punishment: Racial Perceptions of Crime and Support for Punitive Policies. Washington, D.C.: The Sentencing Project

[xxix] https://www.aljazeera.com/news/2020/04/critically-ill-covid-19- uk-patients-bme-backgrounds-200407143303604.html

[xxx] https://www.theguardian.com/world/2020/apr/08/its-a-racial- justice-issue-black-americans-are-dying-in-greater-numbers-from- covid-19

[xxxi] https://www.theguardian.com/world/2020/apr/08/its-a-racial- justice-issue-black-americans-are-dying-in-greater-numbers-from- covid-19

[xxxii] https://www.citylab.com/equity/2020/03/coronavirus-immunity- racism-history-disease-yellow-fever/607891/

[xxxiii]https://www.biblegateway.com/passage/?search=1+Peter +2%3A 9&version=NIV

[xxxiv] https://edition.cnn.com/2019/11/03/us/missing-children-of-color- trnd/index.html

[xxxv] See Seong-Jae Min & John C. Feaster, Missing Children in National News Cover-age: Racial and Gender Representations of Missing Children Cases, 27 COMM. RES. REP. 207, 209, 213 (2010), p 231

[xxxvi] Indirect racism is the art of using prejudice to project and uphold unjust practices against another race purely based on the colour of their skin. This is seen readily, with longer prison sentences for black people, committing the same crimes as white people

[xxxvii]https://www.nytimes.com/interactive/2019/08/19/magazine/histo ry-slavery-smithsonian.html

xxxviii https://www.globalresearch.ca/the-prison-industry-in-the-united- states-big-business-or-a-new-form-of-slavery/8289

xxxix https://boingboing.net/2013/08/06/judge-who-accepted-private- pri.html

xl Webb, Gary (August 18–20, 1996). "Dark Alliance". San Jose Mercury News. Archived from the original on December 20, 1996

xli Webb, Gary (August 18, 1996). "America's 'crack' plague has roots in Nicaragua war". San Jose Mercury News. Archived from the original on December 20, 1996. Retrieved February 5, 2015

xlii EPI analysis of Bureau of Labor Statistics Local Area Unemployment Statistics (LAUS) data and Current Population Survey (CPS) data

xliii https://www.epi.org/files/pdf/157382.pdf

xliv Einzig, Paul (1949).Primitive Money in its ethnological, historical and economic aspects. Eyre & Spottiswoode. London. p. 151

xlv Rees, Alun (2000). Manillas. Coin News. April 2000. ISSN 0958- 1391. p. 46–47

xlvi Humanities, National Endowment for the (June 18, 1921). "The broad ax. [volume] (Salt Lake City, Utah) 1895–19? June 18, 1921, Image 1". ISSN 2163-7202. Retrieved October 23, 2019.

xlvii Basing history, circumstances and truths around European culture and history as the superior, dismissing the wider view of the world

xlviii https://www.britannica.com/topic/education/Education-in- British-colonies-and-former-colonies

[xlix] Fola Kareem Olajoku – "Nigeria: The Omoluwabi Terminology"

[l] https://www.britannica.com/topic/education/Education-in-British-colonies-and-former-colonies

[li] https://www.trtworld.com/opinion/should-the-term-black-to- describe-people-of-african-origin-be-retired-29105

[lii] Ligali, March 2005, African History Newsletter

CPSIA information can be obtained
at www.ICGtesting.com
Printed in the USA
LVHW030824281122
733859LV00015B/1262

9 781398 430181